# STREET MECHANIC

The Preachers Son

First Edition

Copyright ©(add date) The Preachers Son

Written by The Preachers Son

# TABLE OF CONTENT

# PROLOGUE

My book cover starts my story , each one of the eleven clipart pictures have a special meaning in my life and in this book . Below you can see what the clipart represent.

One of our fight got mama caught in the middle, we were fighting in the bedroom. I don't remember which one of us ran out of the room and the other threw a wrench. It hit our mom right over her eye as she was talking to my older sister on the sofa. I remember her grabbing her head as she got up, we froze

Oct 26, 1976, a day I will never forget. It was my father's 45th birthday. Me and Otis had been out in Southland riding his motorcycle with my 1st cousin and some other guys from school. We got back to my house and as we pulled into the drive way some little kids from the neighborhood came running up to me and said that my mom was gone to take my dad to the hospital

I had hit him in the head, with a hoe when we were younger in a fight in which he had something to hit me with but I was faster with the hoe. He still has the scar in his head. Another time, he had broken a coke bottle in my back when he hit me with it. Back then the bottles were glass.

Being a mechanic is a very dangerous job. I don't care how good you are. Safety should be the first thing on your mind before you touch or attempt to repair a vehicle. You need to know if it's in a safe place to be worked on. Is the engine hot? Do you have to jack it up? Do you have jack stands? Do you have gloves to protect your hands? Do you have the right tools? And do you know what you're doing?

He said, everything depended on the arresting officer, it was her call. I'm thinking damn I am gone, because she is kind of big and look like one of the women in the Russian commercial modeling uniforms and she didn't look too happy

I finally went to doctor and got a call when the test came back that they wanted to see me ASAP, and had already made an appointment for the next day

The light was covered with bees. They had turned it into a beehive, but these were not honeybees. They were all over the light. Otis said, "Tell her she needs to call somebody to get them bees, and then we will change the light." I look at him and said, "She did call somebody. Us!"

I didn't think much until I saw the look in Otis eyes though the rearview mirror. Then I saw that the guy had a gun in his hand and it was pointed at Otis .He was looking at the gun as the guy told him to get out. I had not seen many hand guns and all I knew it was big and black. Otis didn't move he didn't know what this was about and neither did I.

On the way to school one morning in daddy's 59 Chevy, we went around a curve and crashed into Papa's truck. He was on his way to our house. I remember being thrown forward and daddy telling us to get out.
    Papa was already out and at the car door making sure we were ok.

The time was here. I got my lady to drive my van. I opened the sunroof. We rode past the house so I could show her which one. I got in the back, so I could stand up in the roof. We

went down two blocks so we would not have to turn on North Street. We set at the stop sign looking at the house for about a minute. I told her to just go like normal and that I would get only one shot.

To read there was always Sears, JC Penney's or a Wards catalogue, which was also the toilet paper. We also had wasp nests to deal with sometimes

# INTRODUCTION

I often tell friends about my days with GENERAL MOTORS and stories about working on the assembly line. In addition, stories about being a mechanic using the knowledge I learned over the years. I decided to take my first year retired to write a few lines about how it was through the eyes of a 19 year old fresh from the south. General Motors, was founded in 1908,

My clock at GENERAL MOTORS starts at 4pm June 22, 1979 on a summer evening.

I don't know what happen to cause GM to fall so far in debt, and it has nothing to do with the writing of this book. I never went to any board meeting on the running of GM. I have never worked on that level. I was a line assembly UAW worker for all my 30 years

In My opinion, the real story of GM can never be told. No one person knows it all with hundreds of thousands of UAW workers spanning over decades, in dozens of plants all over the world. Everyone will have a different story. All the way from the workers on the line, to the white collar workers. Some people will see things that they can relate too, other have never worked on this level will be surprised. This was life as I saw it during the time I was there. This book is not just about GM, it is about my life at GM and, where it has taken me in 30 yrs.  It is also not meant to be my life story, but just some highlight of my 30 years at GM.

Working at GENERAL MOTORS was more than just a job. It turned into a family, and a learning career. Also working at GM help me to take what I learn over 30 years and take it to the streets.

At 50 yrs old, I am at the end of my 30 years with GENERAL MOTORS. What started out as a job, ended as a learning experience that took me through history, where I learned more about cars than I would  anywhere else. I have worked in 14 GM plants in four states. I have spent most of my time on the line in hundreds depts. I have been the repairman, the relief man, and anything else they wanted me to do.' I have worked in rain and snow, and in the hot sun. The longest I spent on any one job was about three years, in any one plant Buick eighteen years.

I have had more layoffs than I can remember. My hands have swollen so big; I could not get gloves on at times. I have had pain in all parts of my body with two operations on my arm and, was out most of my last year.

I have made many friends and have had some good and bad times.

As I think back over the years, and how they went so fast, I can remember some days as if it was yesterday. Other days I just want to forget, as if they never happened. There were days that I wanted to quit and never go back. If it had not been for my Aunt Willie Mae in the 1st year I might have.

I saw 30 years of changes at GM and saw people come and go .It's hard to work next to someone for years and not get to know them and their families. I was there in the good years when most GM plants were on overtime to keep up with the demands for GM products and in the years when most dealers were overstocked, and plants were lying off with no recall date in sight.

When the foreign car companies took the number one spot, it took GM from the top of the big three to an unknown position in the auto world.

There is no one reason why GM lost the number one position, but from the inside, it seems that the foreign companies moved to take a big part of the market. With smaller cars, longer warranties, and their labor cost being less than GMs; it may take a few years but I do see GM at the top again.

As I drive the highways now and see a GM car or truck that came from a plant that I have worked in, I wonder if my fingerprints are in it somewhere. I was working with a company that kept not only America, but also the world rolling with cars and trucks for many years.

I know that the days of old school ways at GM are gone forever. Most GM supervisors do not work their way up from the line like they did in 1979 and before I was hired. Now they come right out of school, some have never even been in a plant before, but their degree says they can do the job. There was only team work at GM because it took teams of workers to build anything coming down a GM line, no matter what we are building

Having a job at GM meant a lot of unknowing about whether or not you will be called back to work from layoff. Unknowing about whether the plant will have work for the next few years or more. Unknowing weather you will have to move to keep your job. It did mean medical benefit and good pay and as a job it was at the top. There is nothing bad I can say about working at GM. To some it was just a job; to me it was 30 years of school. Taking what I learned at GM over the years to the streets help make me a STREETMECHANIC to most that know me and call on me.

When l went home for Christmas 2014 my mom asked me about finishing my book. I told her that I would soon; I just wish she was still here to see it. Anyone can follow their dream, if they wake up. If I can do it anybody can do it.

As I said, I am a mechanic not a writer. I don't know how to type, so this is all 2 and 3 finger work done by me on my laptop. I plan to release this book unedited in my own words. Life to me is not edited by anyone and neither were my 30 years. Any mistakes you may find I take full blame. And you may find a few words misspelled, some periods missing or too many commas, but I do believe you will get the message. I thank GOD for what I learned. I hope you enjoy my story.

# "3 ME"

"My twin brother and I were born in a small town called Marianna, Arkansas, eleven days into 1960. We left Marianna the next day. Years later when we drove through town mama showed us the little white house we were born in. I thought we were born in the hospital down the road. We were born at the doctor's house clinic. We were the third and fourth kids, which would later become ten. We didn't live in the town, but on a small farm between the Marianna and the Mississippi river, in a town called Southland, which was just about all farmland.

Our mom was from Rondo, but had gone to school in Marianna. She went to school with the family of the Chambers brothers, long before anyone knew what crack was. She had met and married our dad and our family began in Southland, Arkansas.

We lived on Wire Rd. It was deep in the country and our grandparents lived across the field about half a mile away, before they moved to Lexa, Arkansas. We had a few chickens and pigs. Our grandpa had two mules a cow, pigs, chickens, and two dogs named Butterfuff and Dittybate. We had a few neighbors and we went to Pleasant Hill Missionary Baptist Church which was about 3 miles away on a hill, it has since fallen down. There's an old lady named Mrs. Bessie that taught us how to fish, her daughter had been married to my mother's baby brother years before my time, and now they live together down the road from us. Another lady name Miss Pearl, lived on the corner, she was always sending money to Rev. Ike.

There was an old couple that lived in a white house down a small road behind our house, Mr. Hike and Mrs. Minnie. He was the first person I knew to die. There were 2 white families the Clifton's brothers and their kids. I think they owned the land we lived on.

We liked going to my uncles in Rondo because they had a pond with fish, snakes, frogs an apple tree. He also had two kids at that time that were younger than I was. He let us help kill hogs sometimes, which was cool but all work. Once he killed a big male hog, after the hog was dead we had to scrape and pull the loose hair off. The hog is placed in a barrel hot water to help with the hair and cleaning before being hung up by the hind legs and cut open. My uncle cut the nuts off, washed off the blood, and threw them in the fire.

One of our jobs was to get the shit out of the chitterlings. When they were cut out of the hog after its hanging up, along with lots of other parts, this was an all day job. After about an hour my uncle got a stick and dragged the hog nuts out of the fire. After letting them cool a minute he cut one in half and sliced off us a peace to taste, not bad, but I prefer ham.

When we were 19 months old, my older sister and brother were outside with my twin and me. I am not sure who was watching who, but somehow my twin managed to slip away into the field. The crop was over his head. Mama told us years later about it. How she had went out to look for him alone and not finding him before going for help. She told us how the whole area was being searched and they had to drain a few wells. I only remember mama sitting next to our wood burning stove crying. I am not sure that time was connected to him being lost. I was only nineteen months old too. It was said that a sock or a shoe was found the first night, but they didn't tell mama. He was gone for two days and two nights before somebody found him. Years later my twin went to Helena World paper office and found the story of the missing Negro boy who was found eating elderberries. To this day, we still run into some of the older people that helped search. They usually ask us which one of us got lost.

When we were about seven, we were on the way home from school. Mama started talking about Dr. King. Not sure what she was saying about him, but I remember asking why they called him doctor if he was a preacher? She said he was a black preacher. He was helping black people. I don't remember her telling us about his death thinking we may be too young to understand. I don't remember hearing that name before that day in 1967; I think that was the day he died. There were two white boys down there name randy and jay, they were our age but never played with us, we did see them driving their fathers' truck and tractor.

Our grandpa used to dig wells around the area, there was no running water. You had to have a pump or a well, or a neighbor that did have water. Our out house or "bathroom" was about 100 feet behind the house, about the size of a phone booth with a top, door and a bench, with a hole to sit on. To read there was always Sears,

JC Penney's or a Wards catalogue, which was also the toilet paper. We also had wasp nests to deal with sometimes.

Papa didn't play much and one day he was pulling up buckets of water from our well pouring them into containers he had in the back of his truck. My twin and I were on the other side of the well seeing who would be the first to stick their fingers in the bucket as it came up. He had asked us to stop once or twice but we didn't. The next bucket came up we held our hands out waiting on the bucket to get close. Just before the bucket reach us Papa pulled it up and poured it over our heads. We took off running. Being wet was not a problem, mama finding out we didn't listen to Papa would be a problem. So we kinda hid out till we dried out.

Whenever we went to Lexa with daddy he gave us a quarter each if he stopped at the store by the tracks, we got a soda and chips. One day on the way home from school, daddy told us that our Uncle Jesse, my mama's baby brother, would pick us up and takes us to his house in Rondo. Our house had burned down. My twin and I were in the back seat of his 59 Impala and we just looked at each other not saying a word. The house was coming up; we could see the big tree that was at the driveway to the house. When daddy made the turn it was all gone. The house was still smoking; the chimney was the only thing standing. I could see the stove and refrigerator; they were black, standing in the ashes. The barn and the tractor were fine, so was the outhouse. A small part of the pig pen was burned because it was close to the house. Daddy had put a board across the spot to keep the pigs in and the chickens were all over the yard, as they always were. There were a few people around. I don't remember who they were, but I remembered Uncle Jesse Picking us up and going to his house. Mama was there along with the smaller kids and my older brother who didn't go to school that day, Mama also had a newborn. I am not sure which one of my little sibling it was.

We stayed with them a few days then we moved to the house my grandparents had moved out of. My grandpa still had the animals there along with his potato house, where he stored sweet potatoes in a shack that was half underground and had to be \kept dark and cool. That was very scary for a nine year old. Papa always kept dark and cool. Papa always kept a Bible and a shot gun in his truck. If he saw a stray dog on his land he'd pulled out the gun and takes a shot at it. I never saw him hit anything. I don't really think he tried.

He would always ask us the same riddle, how to spell hard water with three letters. For some reason I think he thought we forgot the answer is ice.

Dust on the road let you see for miles if cars are coming, but the biggest danger was the curves. On the way to school one morning in daddy's 59 Chevy, we went around a curve and crashed into Papa's truck. He was on his way to our house. I remember being thrown forward and daddy telling us to get out.

Papa was already out and at the car door making sure we were ok. Daddy told us to walk the rest of the way to the bus stop as him and Papa look at the wreck. Later that day, mama called the school to see if we were ok. A few weeks later, daddy had the white "59" Impala back good as new.

Daddy had a new house built in West Helena, Arkansas. Mama told us about the neighborhood and how all the houses are in a row and the floors are cement. It has 3 bedrooms and an inside bathroom. We couldn't wait to move.

# "4.THE EARLY YEARS"

My first job that I can remember was not house work, but working in the cotton fields chopping cotton next to my mother for $4 a day. This was a start to hard work, which I would end up doing a lot of along with my brothers. I didn't mind working. It all depended on the kind of work, which depended on the season. Summer was the hardest. We also played as much as we worked sometimes more. We played when we worked, as long as daddy didn't catch us. He was all about work when it was time for working.

My father became a Church Of God In Christ (COGIC) preacher in the early 70s. We went to church a lot; three or four times a week and twice on SUNDAY. People say preacher's kids are bad but my parents didn't have that problem. We knew that no adult had better not tell anything on us, because there would be no questions just ass beating.

Daddy always seems to be working on something most times around the house. He always used Craftsman tools. We used to sneak into his toolbox and get what we wanted and tried to put it back before he needed it. I think he knew but never said anything

Daddy worked at Faust saw mill on Russell St. He had been working there as long as I can remember. It was one of 2 lumber mills in town. He also worked at the cotton gin at night in Southland in the fall. He drove the church bus and kept it running. He had also put the motor in it, even before he started to preach. He was not a big drinker, but he smoked cigarettes daily. Then one day he just put the pack away and was deep in church and took us all with him. We joined a small COGIC Church in Lexa, AR; where we just about doubled the congregation. My father was the assistant minister a few years after being there.

We moved to West Helena in 1970. When we moved there, the city was under a boycott at the strip mall. I never knew what it was about or when it ended all I knew was we got our first house with an indoor toilet. We were moving up! But still; we worked the land we grew up on. We had a crop of something there every year. We had to plant, weed and pick when the time came. We also did work on other farms in the area; chopping cotton was the main summer work.

We grew cucumbers by the acres for a few years. Then we started to grow okra which was a little better because there was no bending and it was not as heavy. But I still didn't like it or any other farm work. I had to do my part if I wanted to eat. And because it was what we were told to do, and we never argued about any kind of work; we just did it.

Sometimes on Saturday we would go pick vegetables with papa and load up his truck and he ride through the streets very slow, blowing his horn yelling out what he had to sell as we rode on the back with whatever he had.

We spent most of our time with our mom because daddy was always working. She took us to the fields most of the time. She drove daddy's truck sometimes. One day on the way to the farm, I noticed her shifting the gears in the truck. I could not figure out how she knew what gear to put the truck in. After we got to the field and started working she stopped to rest; I asked her. As she sat on the ground, I asked how you know where the gears are on the truck. She picked up a stick and drew the letter H on the ground, then she put 1 2 3 R. one number at each point at top and a number and the letter R at the bottom. Then she told me how to put my foot on the clutch and gas, and when I feel the truck move as I lift my foot off clutch to give it more gas till truck starts to roll, then push clutch and pull stick to 2, then down to 3 as truck pick up speed. To back up just push clutch and put stick on the R at the bottom of the H.

Then she gave me the keys and said to try it. I got the keys and went to truck. I had the stick in my hand I drew a big H on the ground next to the driver's door on the ground and put the numbers and letter on it just like she had did. I got in the truck and pushed the clutch down and started to shift the gears. I could feel the H, mom was talking about and I shifted until I knew what gear I was in. then I put the key in and started the truck. I had my foot pushing so hard on the clutch that my leg was stretched all the way out. I had the other foot on the brake and I put the truck in first gear and slowly started to lift my foot off the clutch and the truck rolled about three feet. I was so happy all I could do was smile; I put the truck shifter on the R and backed the truck back where it was. Mama never said anything but I know she was looking. Years later whenever any of her kids got their driver's license, we became her driver just about everywhere she went.

At that time it was just the three oldest boys that did most of the work in the fields. We also did just as much running around the neighborhood doing just about whatever we wanted long as we knew not to get into trouble or go too far. We spent most or out time at the country store ran by Katy and Doc. We played pool in the back, they also had, one pinball machine, and a juke box. The place was small but it was close to home. All the kids from the subdivision hung out there. My mother was not crazy about us being there, but there were a lot worse places we could have spent hours. To this day I don't think anyone ever got killed or shot there, but there were fights all the time and the next day or so all was good. I remember the only way they would cash a twenty is if you were spending most of it. But if they were going to give you change they had to go in the back and get it. This was also where they lived with two big black dogs. Katy always talked about her kinfolks in Michigan and how they always coming to see her. They did come down years later and I got to meet them.

We were too young to hang out at Places like the ABC cafe on Plaza Street; also called the line. Or the Brick house Lounge in Southland. They always seem to be jumping when we passed on our way to church.

Around 1975 my brothers and I would build and tear up anything. We would take just about any wheels and build go-carts and stick shacks also slingshots out of wire or tree branches. We also would fix bicycles, and went on to minibikes and motorcycles, cars came much later. My older brother had gotten his first car that summer. He had asked daddy about getting a new bicycle since he had a job after school. Daddy told him to save for a car. He was thrilled and started looking at cars in books. Showing me and my twin pictures of Corvettes and others sports cars that he was thinking about getting. Few weeks later dad brought home something like a 67 Impala. He treated like it was a vet and then he got to take us to the farm to work.

He spent a lot of time with one of our cousins that were our age. He was always finding some kind of hustle to make money. They had lived in West Helena for years but had brought a house in Southland not too long ago. My dad had gotten onto my older brother when him and my cuz missed school and went to cut grass. My cuz had been having trouble with his mower and got pissed at it. He kicked it when it was running. His foot went under the mower and his big toe was cut off. Daddy was pissed; he told my brother he had better never miss school again. I guess since he was about 16 he was too old to whip so daddy just fussed a little and my brother got the point. My twin and I clowned my cuz for years about having nine toes, even today.

I had started hanging out with a guy named Odis when I was in the 10th grade and he became like another brother in my family , He lived in Helena about 5 miles from me, but he had a car and a motorcycle. We were together every chance we got, he taught me how to ride a motorcycle and I also learned how to drive his ford pinto four speed stick in the floor. I already knew how to drive a column shift truck.

Oct 26, 1976, a day I will never forget. It was my father's 45th birthday. I and Otis had been out in Southland riding his motorcycle with my 1st cousin and some other guys from school. We got back to my house and as we pulled into the driveway some little kids from the neighborhood came running up to me and said that my mom was gone to take my dad to the hospital. I hopped off the back of the motorcycle and told Odis I will get with him later and went in the house. My three little brothers and two of my sisters were at the dinner table about to eat. I asked my sister what happened. All she knew was mom and my twin brother had gone to see about daddy. She thinks them at the hospital. I didn't know what to do, so I called the Helena hospital, up on the hill by our high school. It was the only hospital in town.

When the nurse answered I gave his name and asked if he was there or anyone from my family. A minute or so had past, Sis. Taylor, one of our church members, came on the phone. I asked, "How's daddy". All I heard was your daddy is dead. I said, "Where is mama?" She said that she was on her way to my grandparents' house with the pastor to inform them. I hung up the phone. I came back in the kitchen and told the kid's daddy was dead. My baby sister started to cry. I am not sure they knew what I was saying. I stood there for a minute, and then I called my oldest brother who was working at KFC at the time. I told him daddy was dead. He yelled, "Whose daddy? "I told him ours. The phone went dead as I found out later he ran out door and headed to hospital.

My next call was to my cousin that I had been riding with just minutes before. His mom is my dad's sister and when he picked up the phone he started to joke about leaving me and Otis in the dust when we were on the motorcycles. I cut him off and told him daddy was dead and the phone went dead. I could hear my baby sister still crying in the kitchen. I heard a car sliding to a stop in front of the house; it was my cousin and his mom. He must have been flying to get there so fast. They were getting out when I came out of the house and asking me, "What happened? I still had no idea what had happened. All I knew was he was dead. We jumped in the car and went to hospital and still did not find out anything except he was there and had died.

By the time we got back to the house mama was back, and before long the house was full of people from the church and the neighborhood. Mama had been planning a birthday party for that night. She said, "I'm glad your daddy went to bed so I can make his cake." The cake was still on the kitchen table. He had opened the card and read it. He took out the $10 that mama had put in it. He had given mama a kiss before he went to work as he did every morning. He had also gotten a birthday card from my oldest sister that day. She had gotten married the year before and was in Germany with her husband that was in the army. In the card was the news of his first grandchild that was born the following year. She was a little firecracker and still is today.

This was a big blow for mama she had just buried her father the past July. He died in our bedroom from a stroke and it was his car that daddy was working on at the time of the accident.

I found out later that evening that when he got off work he had went to work on a car that he was keeping under a friend's barn. He was working under the car when the jack slipped and the car fell on him trapping him under the car. No one knows how long he was there, but his friend found him when he got home and called my mother and 911 after he jacked the car up and pulled him out. By the time the EMS got there, there was nothing they could do. My grandfather came over the next day. He didn't say much I remember him just walking around the back yard not really looking at anything like he was in a daze. I could tell that he was having a hard time accepting daddy death. Grandma was in the house with mama and some more church members.

People had been coming and going all night and the house always seen to be full. The one thing I knew for sure was the rest of the family was coming home very soon. My dad had a lot of sisters and a younger brother and they're all up North except Aunt Frances, she had been over and was staying very close to grandma. His funeral was on Halloween. It was the biggest our church had ever had. It was the first time I had seen so many people packed in our small church. The cars were parked about a mile on each side of the road and there were people all out the doors. There were a few white men there and I think one was his boss from the mill. He had gotten up and talked about how good of a worker daddy was and how he was always offering to look at broken down machines at the mill that he had never seen before. They called him the repair man. He was buried about a mile from the house in the cemetery across the road from where he was killed. I still look that way every time I pass there if I don't stop and visit him.

My best friend Otis had lost his father less than a year later before we finished high school. We were working at the Tribune newspaper across the street from the West Helena Fire Station. The phone in the office rang and it was for him, which was odd because nobody knew we were there or so we thought. It was his mom she had been trying to track him down and remembered he had told her he was going to stuff papers with me. She had found one of the papers in the trash, got the number and called the office. After she told him, he then told us and all my memories of daddy started to come back. I am glad he was with me that day and now I was with him. He didn't want to leave so we just finished working talking very little and went home later that day. It was years later, one day when I went to visit daddy's grave and he was with me that we found out that our fathers are buried less than twenty feet apart, along with his older brother that was killed about two years before on a motorcycle.

My mother never missed a beat with us. I think she knew if one of us got out of hand because daddy was gone we would all try it, so she seem to be a little harder on us about doing what she said to do. One of the big problems, she had from me and my twin was fighting. We would fight about anything, all the time. I had hit him in the head with a hoe when we were younger. In a fight in which he had something to hit me with but I was faster with the hoe. He still has the scar in his head. Another time, he had broken a coke bottle in my back when he hit me with it. Back then the bottles were glass.

One of our fight got mama caught in the middle, we were fighting in the bedroom. I don't remember which one of us ran out of the room and the other threw a wrench. It hit our mom right over her eye as she was talking to my older sister on the sofa. I remember her grabbing her head as she got up, we froze. I could see a small knot rising over her eye. I am sure mama didn't know how to cuss; or was just that saved that she kept her tongue. She didn't say much, this was not a time for her to send us out for a switch so she could whip us. This was a rare time when she grabbed the 1st thing she saw. The next thing I knew she had a toy plastic ball bat in her hand. She was hitting us both at the same time and it didn't matter where the bat landed to her. We were all over the floor and knew the last thing we could do was run or leave that room before she was done with us. I don't remember too much more that happen that day, but I do remember what she did to cut our fighting down a whole lot a few months later.

We had gotten into another fight about something and mama had us to stand in front of her with a belt in her hand till we hugged and kissed. We were not having that and tried to stand our ground. I knew we were going to get a whipping for the fight anyway so why I gotta kiss him, but after a few hits at first we got a little closer until our faces almost touched. Mama had to grab the back of our heads and push us together to get us to kiss. Then she still hit each of us with the belt a few times for fighting and not doing like she said to do.

Our mom was kinda quiet outside the house; she never drank, smoked or cursed. Most of the yelling she did was at us for something we did. I have only seen her get into a yelling match once in my life, and that was over her kids. One day she had sent one of us to the Country Store to get something. I don't remember what it was, but they came back with the wrong change. Mama sent them back to the store and Katy was not giving anything back. After going back home telling mama what Katy said, she headed to the store walking with three or four of her kids following her along with a few other kids. She was not mad at the time because she thought it was just a misunderstanding, but Katy claims her child must have lost the money. My mom knew better and threw everything on the counter and wanted all her money back. The next thing I knew they were yelling back and forth. We were standing outside the door. We had known Katy and Doc for years and really liked them, but this was my mama first time being there. And it was also her last. They only yelled at each other and I am glad the counter was between them because if it came to blows Katy would not have a chance. Mama had nine kids at the time and was in good shape from working in fields and keeping us in line.

After a few minutes of yelling Katy threw her money on the counter, mama got it, and we all headed back home. On the way back she told us never to go back in there. That was crushing to hear. That was the only place that was close and safe for the younger kids in the area. Katy was like another mom to a lot of the kids. She kept the kids in order and was always saying she was going to tell parents if their kids acted up or band them from the store for a few days. After a few days, we ended up sneaking back in to shoot pool and even though Katy had had a big run in with our mama, it didn't seem to matter. She just kept being Katy and years later she joined our church. I don't think she even remembered the run in with mama back in the 70s.

# "5. HIGH SCHOOL AND OUT"

After losing daddy, we did not farm the land anymore. My brothers and I found other ways to make money around town. We picked up pecans, sold newspapers, cut grass and spent a lot of time in cotton fields. My mother had gotten a job at Bobby Brooks, a clothing plant behind the ice house on Plaza St. I spent a lot of time with Otis; I learned how to ride his motorcycle. I got to be good at driving his blue Pinto, with the stick in the floor. He had painted a big ass horse head on the hood of the car with white barn paint. It covered the whole hood. He said it was a Pinto, but didn't even look like a horse to me.

He was the only person mama didn't mind me hanging out with. No matter how long I was gone, sometimes it would be days. Long as, I told her I was with him, it was ok. His mother felt the same about me because we were together so much. We never really got into anything that I would call serious trouble, but we did have some fun.

I remember my first time going to the movies on Cherry Street at the movie theater we went see "which way is up", Richard Pryor. Otis had a Richard Pryor 8 track that we listened to sometimes, but it was my 1st time seeing him like this, we also hung out at the park over the levee in Helena or on the Mississippi Riverbanks.

One day, he was telling me about a nice lady he had met at the principal's office, when he was getting send home for something. He could not remember her name but she was meeting him after school in the parking lot to take her home. Since she lived on my side of town, he would drop me off at home. We were in parking lot waiting on her, when he looked and said here she comes. I looked the way he pointed, three or four girls were walking towards us. Two of them I didn't know I think they were in the 11th grade. One of the girls, I knew from church. She and her sister had ridden the church van, when my father drove it. She was walking toward us I thought she was coming over to speak to me like she always did because daddy had been gone less than a year.

As she got closer, he got up and met her. He picked her up, swung her around, gave her a kiss, and a hug. When he put her down, she smiled at me and said," Hey twin!" He said," Y'all know each other?" I said, "Yea, she go to our church been knowing of her for years." "This the girl you been telling me about?" I asked. I laughed, the one thing I knew about her was that she had a temper that got hot very fast, as he would find out later. She was not into his games. The day he met her she was checking out of school to go to court for hitting a girl in the head with a bottle. Instead of it being me and him going everywhere, it was me him and her.

We spent a lot of time in Lambrook, a country town on the other side of Lakeview, Arkansas. That's where he was born and went to school before moving to Helena. His family had about forty acres of land with a three bedroom trailer house on it. That was empty and in ok shape. For seventeen and eighteen year old boys, we had a lot of freedom and most of it was about making money. We spent most of the summer of"77 at that trailer, we had no water the first two days because when we turned it on the water came from everywhere. We found about ten cracks in the pipes that we had to keep plugging them up until we could turn on the water. We only had cold water; we never got the water heater working.

One night, we were hanging out at the country store by my house. Otis had never really spent a lot of time there. He didn't know a lot of the people. We were supposed to pick up Mindy. I had a lady friend that we were also picking up at the store. We had planned to get a room with the girls. As we sat in his Pinto, he got in the back seat and my lady friend got in front passenger seat. I had been driving his stick but still had trouble with it sometimes. As we sat in the car about to go, Otis was pissed that Mindy was trying to argue about something. She had walked across the park headed home. He said," Let's go, I will go by her house and get her later." I started the car and was about to back out when somebody opened the passenger door from outside. It was one of the older boys that lived on my street. I had seen him and a group of guys walk up and they were standing near the driver door. I didn't think much until I saw the look in Otis eyes through the rearview mirror. Then, I saw that the guy had a gun in his hand and it was pointed at Otis. He was looking at the gun as the guy told him to get out. I had not seen many hand guns and all I knew it was big and black. Otis didn't move he didn't know what this was about and neither did I.

The guy said something about not giving them a ride earlier that day when they were trying to hitch a ride to Helena. I remember when we had passed them, but we passed a lot of people standing by the liquor store trying to get to Helena. They were mad because we didn't give them a ride and it had come to this. The guy backed away from the car and told Otis to come on out. Otis was not getting out. The guy stood in front of the car with the gun stuck in the front of his jeans, with his hand still on it.

Otis was begging me to run the guy over. I said," hell no he will shoot all of us." He kept telling me that all I had to do was give the car a lot of gas and jump off the clutch. I reminded him that I can't. I was scared. The cement blocks in front of store will stop the car. He will kill us. He then begged me to run to my house and get my gun. I only had a 410 gauge shotgun and that was no match for anything shooting back. I lived about three minutes away, if I ran. I was not getting out of the car. The guy had told me to turn the motor off. We sat there looking at the guy and the gun, which he was making sure we could see it. After what seem like an hour, may have been about ten minutes I looked out window, the guys older brother was walking up to the rest of the guys that were waiting for some kind of action. He talked to them for a minute and called his brother over. We couldn't hear what they were saying and after a few minutes the brother waved his hand for Otis to get out and come over. He got out a lot faster than I thought he would. I kept my seat. They didn't call me. If I needed to get out I would know when.

They talked for a few minutes with the big brother standing next to his brother, who still had the gun in his belt. I don't know what was said but after about five minutes of talking and some yelling. Otis was crying he was so mad. They shook hands and I got out and walked over to Otis, who was still holding the guys hand. I heard him tell him that if he ever pull a gun on him again he had better use it cause he was going to be ready to take it and make him eat it. I caught his arm and said," Let's go!" I leaned over and said," That he still had the gun." He yelled," I don't give a fuck about him and that gun." Somebody must have ran and told Mindy because she was running across the park toward us.

She asked," If everything was ok?" She saw Otis crying. We never told her everything that happened and they stood hugging for a few minutes. I decided to go home. Otis and Mindy got in the Pinto and he backed out and put the car in drive and threw rocks, dirt, and dust all over the road. The car fished tailed and took off down the road. It took a few minutes for the dusk to settle then I told the girl I was with that I was going home. I left her at the store. After that night, he kept his gun with him just about whenever he came to my neighborhood. It was a 410 gauge too.

That next week we got the girls and went to the Holiday Star Hotel, over by the Big Star grocery store. Otis dropped me and my lady friend off and said they will be back. We stayed alone until about 10:30. When Mindy and Otis got back with a bottle of wine, we passed it around until it was gone. As we got ready to leave, Otis said he was keeping the table in the room and taking it to the trailer house. He also decided he was keeping everything and asked me what I wanted. "Nothing", I said. I knew mama would ask where I got it and it would be my ass. We decided we would take all the shit we could get in the Pinto. Not much room with the two ladies. We loaded up all the bed covers and got everything that was in the bathroom, the lamps, two tables that came apart, he even got the Bible, and pillows. The TV was hooked up to some kind of cable so we didn't touch it. As we put everything in the car there was hardly anywhere to sit. I remember it was about midnight before we pulled out and the old man in the office waved at us as we passed him. We all started laughing and waved back as Otis drove away.

Our senior year was coming and we had a few weeks of summer left. By this time Otis and Mindy had a little boy we called Tiger. I had been dating Mindy's little sister Vella, who also went to our church. She had been a virgin when we started dating and I left her that way. Last, I heard she was married to a preacher and had about ten kids. We still spent a lot of time at the trailer with Mindy and the baby. We had planned to have a big party in the barn one Saturday. We spent all week getting the place ready and ran a string of lights across the barn and hooked up some old speakers we had found.

The Friday night before the party, Mindy had been mad for some reason and had been fussing at Otis all day and that night they really got into it. Mindy wanted to go home right then. It was about midnight, but she started to pack her and Tiger things into the Pinto. We started the thirty mile drive back to West Helena in silence. As we went through the curves in the road going through Lakeview, Mindy said give me my watch. Otis said, "What watch?" She said.

"The watch on your arm." She had given him a watch for graduation. He looked at her, took the watch off and held it out to her. The watch barely touch her hand as it went out the window. Otis kept driving then he slowly looked over and asked in a calm voice if she just threw the watch out the window. She said, "Yep!" and kept looking straight ahead. Otis was pissed. He started to yell about how dumb that was and she could have given it to her little brother or somebody. After dropping her off, he took me home. He said, he will get me early that morning so we could set up for the party that Saturday night.

The next morning he picked me up about 9am and we headed back to Lambrook. On the way we stopped at about ten areas in the road looking for the watch and not finding it. All the curves look alike at night and we knew it was a longshot whenever we stopped, but we tried. We got back to the trailer, moved the rest of the stuff and cut the grass. We were just about ready for the party and all it had to do was get dark, which should be in about an hour. We look down the road; we see dust from a car coming. Not knowing who it is or if they were coming for the party a little early, we just waited until the car pulled up next to the trailer and stopped. The door opened and it was Mindy, she had paid the old man that lived next to her to bring her and Tiger back. She got her stuff out of the car and went into the house. Otis wasn't saying anything he went and picked up Tiger and started to play with him. As she got, the rest of the stuff out of the car, we walked over to the barn with the baby to discuss the change in our plans since it was looking like the trailer was going to be off limits for party guest because Otis ex girl and her family were sure to be there.

The party started and I don't know where all these people came from. The town was very small or so I thought. People, mostly teenagers, were dancing and drinking all over the barn and there was plenty of food. It was also my first time seeing weed being smoked. I didn't smoke any but the scent of it was all over the barn. We had four big cans, with fires going, somehow a few thousand papers we were supposed to deliver ended up in the barn. They made good fires. A few of the ladies asked to use the bathroom and Otis had to go in and see if it was ok with Mindy. She was kool with it. She even ate a little but spent most of the time looking out the window to see who Otis was with.

By the 12th grade, we were still hanging together. We didn't stay at the trailer anymore because of school. We found a lot of odd jobs from landscaping to the newspaper office. Later on, we found out that his mom had gone to school with some of my father's sisters before they moved to Southland years before. The school year went fast and military recruiters were always there trying to get students to join up. I had no interest in any of that, but Otis talked me into going over to Mississippi to take the test. We only did it to get out of class for the day and still get credit for being there.

On the way over, the recruiter gave us some papers to look over. We were looking over the papers when he told us that we need to study the papers good and it will help us on the test. We didn't need any help, we had already decided to fail the test and take the day out of school the day. I looked over the papers a few times; it was just a lot of A B C D like questions, with the correct answer filled out. About five minutes after starting the test, it hit me that this was the same test we were looking at in the car. I just had to remember what was where, but the test was not at all hard. We still passed. I wondered how many more kids got to see the test and answers and used that info to pass the test. Anyway the recruiters kept calling me about joining up when school was out and he was ready to sign me up.

I knew I had to get out of West Helena. My dad's sister had been asking me about my plans and said it would be good if I came to Michigan and got a job in the shop with Uncle Bert. That sounded much better than the Army. I just had no idea what Uncle Bert did at that time.

My mom had remarried and was expecting her 10th child. I was ready to leave and hit it out on my own. She knew I was ready and had asked me to stay until the baby was born. She had also told me that "daddy had a good name and don't mess it up". I worked for the city for a minute cutting vacant lots and picking up trash. My little brother was born September 4, 1978. Four days later, I had saved up enough money to get on that gray dog and get out of town. I filled out my papers trying to get a job at General Motor on September 11, 1978. It would be a start I will never forget.

## "6. NEW START IN MICHIGAN"

By September 1978, I was all set and ready to go somewhere. My twin had joined the Army. I was getting bored and ready to leave. My Aunt Willie had been telling me about the jobs in Flint at the shops. I had never thought about where cars come from and didn't know that's what she meant. It was also, where Uncle Bert worked. I got there Friday. That Monday morning I went with my cousin Winston to fill out a General Motors job application. Winston didn't drive and went everywhere on bicycle or the bus.

He loved the Blues and let everyone know it by singing or playing it just about everywhere he went. He showed me how the bus system worked. If I got lost to catch the DuPont Street Bus and get off on Carpenter Road. I will be home. We also rode bicycles all over Flint. I thought I was in shape until I tried to keep up with him. He was about six years older than I was and in cotton picking shape. It seemed like he knew everybody. His friends were older, and he had a lot of them, mostly women. He had two sisters one was my age and the other was older and worked at General Motors.

While I was waiting on GM to call me, I worked with Winston on all kinds of jobs. He did carpentry work and refinished cabinets. We also went on a tour at the Chevrolet truck plant on van Slyke Road. I was amazed at the way they worked. Everybody doing something different as the truck came down the line. The work didn't look too hard. It wasn't in the sun like the cotton field. I couldn't believe how many people it took to run the line. Some people did seem to be working kinda hard. Others seem to be just sitting around. It took about two hours to completely tour the plant. I couldn't wait to get a job there.

After being in Michigan a few months, I came home one night and my aunt told me to pack a few things because I will be flying to New York the next day. She told me that some of my aunts in New York wanted to see me. I had never been on a plane or even thought about it. Now I had about 6 hours to get ready to fly out. I couldn't sleep so I called my mother and told her about going to New York. She said had talked to my twin and he told her he was in New York.

I knew he was finishing basic training. Then he would be going to Germany soon.

Just about anything we did big we called our mom to tell her. When I got to New York the next morning I found out that they had planned to surprise us. They forgot to tell mama. Soon as I got off the plane I asked, "Where he was?" she laughed. My cousin Fanny asked, "What makes you think he's here?" I talked to mama last night and he must have too.

They had gotten us tickets to see The Wiz on Broadway. This was my first play. This was a big difference from the movie theater on Cherry Street in Helena. He was on his way to Germany for about three years. They wanted us to spend some time together before he left. After all the years of fighting with him I had no problem giving him a hug as he got on his bus when the visit was over. I wiped away my tears. Only after my cousin, Fannie started to cry, as he got on the bus.

I stayed in New York for two weeks staying at different relative's houses until I got back to Flint.

I was nowhere near being prepared for the winter. It snowed in Arkansas but nothing like this. I had never seen a snow plow or road salt. It was so cold that it felt like I was breathing in ice.

I got a job at a ladies clothing store in Genesee Valley. I was up at 6 am to catch a bus to get there by 9 am. This went on for six months. General Motors had called and I had gone to a few orientation classes. In June 1979, I was called to work in the foundry. Buick started a whole new page in my life.

# "7. THE FIRST 90 DAYS"

The first 90 days were hell on lots of folks. Especially if you could not keep up or had a boss trying to drive you like a slave. There were trainers to train you on whatever job you were assigned to. You still had to learn fast to prove you could do it or try. Because they could send you home at any time with less than ninety days. It was all very easy to me I had been working in cotton fields and doing all kind of farm work as long as I could remember.

For the money I would me making I would be happy, I had a love yet to been seen for mechanic work, and what makes a car run and working here was giving me a chance to see and learn more than I ever would in school. It would just be a thirty year lesson.

About 15 people were hired on 6 -22 -1979, that day along with me. We had to wait in a break room until we were taken to our department's one at a time. We hoped and prayed we got good jobs, but we really did not know what a good job was. We had seen people working and we had our foot in the door. We all thought we were ready for whatever they had in store for us to do.

Whatever job you got you had to do it for as many cars as they were going to build that day. If you were putting on tires, you had to put on about 550 in an 8-hour shift. Most jobs have a small list of things to do, and it all has to be done in about a minute because you have to finish before the car passes your work station. Most new hires were out the first week if they got a hard job or just too much work.

I lucked out and went to the foundry where the engine block was poured and only worked with sand molds out of the oven. I thought I was in heaven but with all the hot steel popping, and the heat from the ovens it felt like hell.

My boss took me to this guy and told him to train me on what to do and walked away. The guy had on dark shades and a blue rag around his head, he shook my hand, and we exchanged names. He said I need a hat or something on my head if walking around in that area. He looked at his watch then back at me, and said that I could disappear until 7pm, it was 400: p.m. I looked around and saw a chair, and had a seat. I was not going anywhere tonight.

I sat and looked at him work to see what the job was all about. I asked what I had to do and he said that it was a 2-person job and that the other guy was off that day. He was the extra man in the group. He said that he and I would be doubling up on the job, which meant one of us would do both jobs, while the other took a break. Most time it was hour on hour off. However, it has been done day on day off. Long as the job was done the boss did not give a shit who did it if you were in a laid-back dept.

All we had to do was get the sand molds out of a big ass oven that looks like cooking pizzas. They come out on big belts, one oven for each man. By doubling up one man did the whole job, while the other went home or somewhere to fuckoff. At that time, I found out the line was going a little slow and later found out that at full speed one man could still do it with no sweat. We just had to set the molds on a line called the double A frame line, where they went over to where the metal was to be poured to make the engine block. You had to keep your head covered in that area because sparks were flying everywhere. Fans were blowing dirty air all over the plant; it was the middle of June and about 90 degrees outside.

The job was easy. He told me how it was around the dept. and told me about how doubling up worked; sounded good to me, so I was in for whatever the night may bring. I still stayed in that seat until my time to work.

He asked me, where I was from, I told him Arkansas. He said the old man on the other side of the oven was from Arkansas too. I got up and put on my gloves and picked up one of the molds they were about 40 pounds. Not bad, I was 19 years old and in good shape, I could do this.

I was left alone at 7pm, then about 8pm a little old black guy who was making sure oven temp and primer dip for molds was right came over to meet me. I heard you from Arkansas he said, as he shook my hand, I told him what part, he said, that I should know his people. They were in Lexa, Arkansas a small town off Highway 49. My grandparents had moved there when they moved from Southland in the late 60s. He was right I knew them all. Two of the women I have known since the first grade and his cousin were head of police at that time in my hometown. We laughed and talk about our hometown and the folks we knew. He told me he had been gone from there over thirty years and went home every chance he got and kept in touch with all his folks there. We talked off and on most of the night, years later I worked with his son in Buick City.

I was only 19, as I said and the drinking laws had just gone up to 21. However, it did not matter if you had a GM badge; there were bars and clubs all up and down the street. Plant was on one side of industrial street and everything else on the other side. My first night I went to a bar called the White Eagle, which was across the street from my gate. The woman asked for my I.D. and I show her my badge like the guy trained me said to do. We were on lunch break. I did not really drink but I had a beer and chatted with some other new hires about how their jobs were going. I found out one had quit already, saying this is bullshit and she was not going back in there and was out soon as she got a ride to York St.

Lot of folks knows by the first day if this kind of work is for them or not. There were some cases where a pretty girl may catch a foreman's eye and she gets an easy job; but it won't last long. If you make it past two weeks, you can do the work on mostly any job.

Other than working in the fields, I never worked with lots of folks, and some of them were a real trip. Workers got along good in the group I was in; it was very laid back. If you need help, they helped you as much as you needed but it was kind of automatic that the new hires got the worse jobs in the dept. that nobody wanted to do.

It was dirty and dusty all over the area, and if you blew your nose in a white tissue, it would be black. Working in a foundry caused health problems, I found out the foundry would be closing and moving within 2 years, and the department would be phasing out.

I got good at all the jobs I was put on, as I was hired to fill in for people on vacation, so I moved all over the plant, and learned fast. I also got loaned to other areas. Therefore, I got the chance to help put together the motor from start to finish over time. Learning how the engine works and how to build them. All new hires were hoping to get 90 days in before they get laid off and not have to be called back. It used to be 89 days and out before you got 90 days in and became a full UAW member. Well I got my 90 days in and was then laid-off. For some reason we were glad not to go to work and glad to be off.

Back then, when you were laid-off you could go in the area hire pool and be called to any plant in the area. At that time, there were about ten plants all over Flint. If no Flint plant needed people, you may have to go to a plant that has open jobs in another city or state.

I was off four months and came back to plant 36, in Flint where the motor line is. This was very much different than the foundry with triple the noise. There were air guns everywhere. Most swinging from overhead. Some jobs were done from seats sitting on rails next to the line. The worker would sit all day and put on parts as the motors came down the line, with about four feet to roll either way. Most jobs were done standing by the line and a repair station at the end of each department. If you missed doing a part of your job just yell at the repair man. The motor lines snaked throughout the plant with people working on both sides of the line. What started out as a clean engine block at one end came out a fully dressed motor after going through the maze of workers.

Dealing with a lot of small parts was bad on the hands and mine stayed swollen my first two weeks there. Carpal tunnel was a problem with GM workers long before anyone knew what it was. After a few years a lot of the workers there have had some kind of operation to repair muscle or nerve damage that was caused by the job. Working on the line is not like some jobs where it's something new everyday. When you on the line it's the same thing day after day unless you change to another job. You repeat that process as long as you on your job which may be one hour to thirty years plus.

I was bounced from job to job, sometime being loaned out to 3 or 4 departments in a week until I was put on a job installing pistons. I stayed in that department until I was laid-off again, and soon learned that layoffs come with the job. I would just have to pray and deal with it as all the other GM workers, and hope that GM call me back somewhere soon.

"

# "8. ARRESTED IN CANADA"

One Saturday around 1980 the girlfriend I had at the time decided we would take a ride with one of her other girlfriends. They asked if she and her boyfriend could go with us. We decided to ride up to Canada; it was about an hour and a half away. We all got in my car and made the trip to the tunnel. I was driving as we pulled up to the Canadian border check point. The lady at the booth asked me some questions and everything she asked me, I asked the guy in the back seat. Like, where we going? How long we going to be here? I had been out of Arkansas two years and knew nothing about Canada. She pointed forward, and said to pull over to the left and park my car.

We parked and about three officers came to the car and asked us to get out. They took a quick look in the car, after about three or four minutes they came out with a pair of brass knuckles and a military switch blade knife that my twin had given me. They also had my pack of BC headache power and a one inch 35 millimeter film case that had a small amount of weed in it. I didn't even know it was in the car. It was not even enough to cover the top of the case, which was about the size of a quarter. I didn't really smoke back then and just forgot about it being in the car. They told us to go inside, where we were put into a small room. I could see them moving my car around back through the window to a garage. I am scared as hell but trying to laugh it off, as the four of us sit talking. There is an officer at the sliding glass window and one of the girls asked what's going on?

He says that drugs have been found in the car and we were under arrest as of now. The weapons were also illegal. He said to her weapons, weapons what weapons? I asked. He said something about the knife and the brass knuckles they found. I tried to explain they were not really weapons to me just something my brother had given me, it didn't matter. He also told us that the drug penalty was seven years in prison for bringing anything over there. I really got scared when he said that the owner of the car will be the only one charged, and it was my car.

He said everything depended on the arresting officer, it was her call. I'm thinking damn I am gone, because she is kinda big and look like one of the women in the Russian commercial modeling uniforms and she didn't look too happy. After about an hour she comes in with two other officers, I guess they been tearing up my car. They really don't talk to us much; they take the women one way and the men another. Me and the other guy are taken back into a small room and told to remove everything but underwear. After giving them our clothing they looked though them inch by inch. Then had us pull our underwear down and took a quick look to make sure we were not hiding anything. After being sure we were clean, we were sent back out to the first room .The girls were just coming back too. We sat back down and waited for them to tell us something, it was going into the second hour. The others thought the whole thing was kinda funny, but I was not laughing on the inside.

The officer at the window had said that they could keep my car and give me seven years depending on the lady that stopped me. The laughing from the others was getting on my nerves and my girlfriend and I got in to a small argument that got worse later. After a few minutes the lady came back in and said we are going to send you all back to America. Then they said we are never to return and followed us to the car which they had brought back around. She said to make a U-turn though a gate she pointed to and said not to stop in the tunnel. We got in the car and headed back to freedom. We made it back to the American check point and were waved over to the side. The officers came out and asked what was going on; I told them the story about the Canadian and what the found in my car, for some reason they thought it was funny. They could not hold in their laughter, like it was the funniest thing they ever heard. After I told them the story they asked what they do after that, nothing they put everything back in the car and sent me back here. They what? He says, now they were not laughing at all. They put it back? Let me see he said. I opened the trunk and laid out nice and neat were the knife and the knuckles and the camera film cast next to the BC. He said give me the weed. I gave it to him and he said to get out of here. I got back in the car with the rest of them, who had never got out of the car. The officer came to the window and said that Canada had called them with my car tag and make and said to check me out. He said he had had no idea what was going on until I told him they gave it back so I would be arrested in America. He didn't care about the other stuff and let me keep it and we got the hell out of there.

We drove back to Detroit. I really didn't care what we did I was hungry tired and it wasn't even 12:00. We decided to go get something to eat or they decided I really wasn't talking too much. We stopped and got something to eat and somebody brought up the State Fair was in town and decided to go there. We went to the fair and after we get in I just started to walk around. I didn't see or care which way they went, I was just walking around looking, still kinda pissed with no real reason to be. After walking around for about 30 minutes, I noticed that they had been following me from a distance. I was sitting on a bench when my girlfriend sat down beside me and grab my hand and laid her head on my shoulder just like that the fight was over. We spent the rest of the day at the fair and had a good time despite the bad start of the day. Later on I found out that they been following me at the fair because I was their only ride home back to Flint.

A couple of years later I got a chance to go back with a cousin on a fishing trip to Rice Lake, in Canada. I was scared as hell when we approach the border. I didn't know if they kept a record or not and we were going to cross the bridge this time. This time my cousin answered all the questions and we had no problems getting through, and spent 3 days fishing. Couple years later I rode up with group to a place called Wheels Inn, and crossing the border brought back memories and fear.

# "9. THE UNION"

We had to join the union on the first day of work and sign the membership papers and pay monthly dues. I had learned all about the union at GM and Buick local 599. I had been to the old GM plant where a strike lasted for months back in the day when GM knew they had to deal with the union or not build cars.

The UAW union was formed in 1935, to help the workers get the right pay. Have safe working conditions, and limit the numbers of hours we can work without going into overtime, and guarantee jobs security, health and pensions plans. All GM plants have a local UAW union.

It seems to me that the union as I saw it then had done its job and everything was running fine. They were just taking money out of my check. All I ever saw them do was walk around and answer union rep calls. I never knew that the union was as active as it was until rumors of a strike were in the air. Weeks before, we heard that talks were going bad about something that GM and the union were trying to work out but were not getting anywhere. Everyday there was something in the news about the Buicks talks.

At the time, we were working well and I did not take the talks too serious, even when they gave a strike notice. The headline in the papers just got bigger and I really did not think anything was going to happen.

The rumors came faster and I could tell that something was in the air, and that plant seemed to be running differently. Supervisors were really cracking down on small shit and there seemed to be a lot more union reps calls. The reps never seem to be around at that time. It seems like the management and the union people were taking it personal. Men that had been friends for years at GM some in union some in management were bitter. There was so much tension in the air. It was all business for the union; whatever the fight was about, the union was not going to give in.

Sometime that week the headline of the newspapers stated that the union had given a day and time that the workers would walk out. The news always had more information than we got at the plant.

When I got to work, there were a lot of union reps around, they were updating us on the talks, and that we should get our shit together and be ready to walk around 10 pm. That was about 4 hours away. Now, I knew that shit was going to happen unless they did a last minute deal. We waited and worked; at 10 pm all hell broke loose with yells and screams of lets walk. Strike!

Union reps were coming down the aisles yelling, Strike! Let's walk! I joined the flow of people. Some was with the strike and some just were glad to be off work. I was undecided.

I could see some bright lights at the door and thought that channels 12 or 5 news maybe out there. When I got to the door, it blew my mind. There were big ass news trucks with satellite dishes camped out everywhere, and reporters trying to put a camera in anybody's face that were willing to talk to them. It took a minute to take it all in. I saw my friend Kert; he had two other brothers there too. He was just as shocked as I was. This was our first strike. We had heard about them at other plants and seen them on the news. Now we were at the front line as you can say. Union reps had told us to report to the union hall the next day and get our picket walking time. You just do not show up at the picket line, grab a sign, and walk. There were about eleven thousand people at Buick city alone and thousands more at the rest of the complex. Which was about a mile long, therefore, we had to walk so many hours in shifts.

The strikes signs went up as soon as we were out the door; some people went straight to the street and started walking at the entrance to the plant. That is where the news people all seem to be, trying to get a word with anyone holding a strike sign and get their view on the strike.

Kert and I went over to the parking lot at the liquor store and sat under the big tree. We wanted no part of all the Hollywood shit. After a few minutes, the lot was about full as it always was after work and before. The police were directing traffic near the CNN trucks. It made us realize how big the union was. We stayed until we got bored and had nothing to smoke or drink and went home.

The next day Buick city was at the top of the news all over the country, and the newspaper had "STRIKE" in big letters over half the front page. After reading the paper and looking at all the news on TV. I went over to Kert's we talked about the strike hoping it did not last too long. It was our first big strike and we did not know quite how to handle it. We were both glad to be off a few days. Strike pay is about $100 a week and you have to walk the line, we could not afford to be off long.

We drove to the liquor store and sat in the parking lot like we do before we go in and when we get off. The circus with the news trucks was still going own. There were about 10 people walking the picket line with signs and about another 20 including reporters standing around.

As we sat looking, at a reporter that had driven over, asked if he could talk to us about the strike. He had a camera around his neck and a tape recorder on a notebook pad in his hand. He had already went to a few other cars and had spent some time talking to two white guys I knew from the body shop. We had gotten out of the car and were standing next to a group of guys that hang out there every day.

When we were asked about the interview one of the older guy said, "Hell no get your ass back across the street and talk to them, we don't want your ass writing and taking no pictures about shit on this side of the street." The man had spoken broken English but he seems to get the message; as if he had been told to get lost many times before.

As he got in the car and drove away, we started to crack up laughing as we passed the joints and drink. The old man that had ran the reporter away, said that the unions do not need some asshole like that trying to flash our picture all over the news drinking and smoking. Them damn white boys over there should have kept they mouth shut. I knew he was right about the image of GM, and the white boys had just posed for pictures holding up a beer in each hand. If he wants to talk to somebody, let him go across the street and ask all the questions he wants, he said. When it is my turn to walk with the damn sign, he can talk to me. Now he can leave us the fuck alone. I want to get my head right until my time to grab a sign and walk the damn line, he said. We just sat around the tree with nothing to do. Later, we would spend hours shooting pool at the bar on the corner or at the strip club. Anything to pass the time, but mostly we watched for any signs of the strike to end.

The strike was bigger than anyone thought it would be, because it's not just affected Buick City it was all Buick and they shipped parts to dozens of other plants. Which most do not stock parts but use a just in time system and some had parts to run hours and some days. We were not shipping shit that was not out of the plant by strike time the night before.

The news stations got greats shots of the workers walking the line and holding the signs. They interviewed a lot folks. However, I never saw them at the back gate where trucks were trying to sneak out, and some got flats and broken glass, it was anything but peaceful.

It was then I took notice of the union. Buick city's strike had started to shut down other plants that needed parts from us to run. Not sure how many we shut down but it was a lot. GM was almost at a standstill at most plants. In the end, GM gave the union just about everything they wanted and a signing bonus. Just like that the tension was gone, for now. I don't think GM realized how strong Buick city's union was until the strike and that they could shut down just about all GM North America plants with a strike; they had just done it.

Whatever deal they had made was only good for a few years and I am sure that in that time GM will look at this like a chess game and the next move would be on them to make the best deal for them in the next talks; as it had been done for years and years. Today, Buick City is closed and torn down. "

"GM and the union still fight today. The fights have changed; parts that GM workers used to assemble are being outsourced. Sometime whole sections of the car like the dash or the seats come in already put together. From factories, where they make less than half of what we make and we put these parts together on the assembly line, like the parts to a puzzle."

"Over the years, GM found more and more places to get parts and take more GM jobs. GM also cut back on workers benefits to stay completive with other car companies. They closed some plants as the sales fell over the years giving some workers a chance to move to other states, take buyouts, or retire. They also sold off or discontinued some auto brands, and with the help of the union they try to make sure that UAW workers have a job to go to for years to come. "

"It was hard to get fired from GM. You may get time off for something, but the union always seems get the workers job back after a few months. The one thing you can get fired for is sexual harassment. You can hit a lady in the face and go to jail on plant property, and it's a matter for the police, but you are still working. If you tell her she got a nice ass or say too many sexist related things and she report you. GM will do an investigation and you could be fired. Because GM could be sued, and out of lot of cash if her complaints are not seen to, so unwanted sex talking was a big no no. There was enough sex talk going on anyway so few people got fired that way.

Whatever the problem was the Union was there. The unions did a lot for the worker and still do, but the workers have to use common sense and think outside the box to get the jobs done. They need to take a good look at the people they put in office to make decisions on their job and future. The workers may not have much say so in who ran GM but we all know who run the plants because too many unhappy workers can and have had wildcat strikes and walkouts. They can also run so many cars or trucks down the line that need repairing that there will be no where to put them all."

They have had to give up many benefits it had fought years to get. The union still fights to keeps it members working this time the fights were not just with GM. Foreign car builders have started to take a big part of the auto market and they are getting bigger. GM and the union have to work together to bring down the cost of building vehicles.

I believe that if Americans brought American products it will go a long way in getting GM back on its feet and in the number one place again. GM also has to build cars and truck that America can trust and afford to drive; with low costs and easy to maintain. Before foreign car companies hold all 3 big 3 auto spots.

# "10. BUICK CITY"

I had been at Lake Orion for two years when the rumors started to go around that Buick would be calling all their people back. Those that had been laid off went to other plants. If they wanted to they could come back or they could stay where they were.

Around June 1985, for some reasons tension were high at Lake Orion. This was a new GM plant, near the place, where the Pistons played. It had only been open a few years. We were making the small Cadillac and one or two other cars at the time.

An employee that was suspended had mistaken a young college student for a supervisor. When he came out of the plant, he was shot in the head and died. Not sure, what the beef was with the worker and the supervisor but the wrong man died. Just as with any other job, you never know what's on folks mind and what it take to make them snap. Working here had been more stressful than at Buick City in Flint, and driving forty miles did not help. It was a close door plant and the closest place to get something to eat was about three or four miles away.

This was a lot different than at Buick where food and drinking places were everywhere. There was no doubling up here at all that I know of in any of the departments I was in. Most of the workers had come from other plants. The supervisors were stricter than at Buick and they really cracked down on people missing days. If you missed too many days you went into a program that may lead to being fired; and it's hard to get fired from GM.

I was so ready to get back to Flint. The 40-mile drive the last two years was killing me. Buick City was just seven minutes from home. Buick had been calling about 100 people a week back. I checked every week to see where my name was on the list to call back to Buick, which was my home plant. I finally got the letter asking me if I wanted to come back and took no time going along with about 50 other people.

Kert, his brother and I came back together. Kert and I went to the body shop. It was the startup of Buick City, GM would spend about three hundred million dollars, and it would take about 28,000 workers on two and three shifts to run the largest GM complex at that time.  The fisher body on the other side of town closed; everything was moved to Buick City where bodies could be made at Buick instead of driving them across town where it all can be done at one plant,

The startup was very slow trying to get everything to work together.  We got to pick our own jobs, as this was a new department and Kert and I got off line jobs where five of us made the right wheelhouse, which is the part of the fender where the tire sit in the rear, and fed it to the line.  We worked with three older guys who had followed their job from their old plant.

We did not do much because we had nothing to work with for weeks at a time; we had to wait for bodies to come from underbody so we can build them up with the side frames, sometime we had to wait for other depts. to use what we had so our line would move.  We were on 11 ½ hour shifts at the time and I had to be there at 6 pm, and got off at 6 am. There were churches with daycare, bars, and strip clubs on the other side of the street and they were all making money.

I remember before direct deposit on pay day, you could go to just about any bar or liquor store to cash a GM check in Flint.  On payday the wives of some of the guys, sometimes with kids, were waiting by the gate to get the check, before he blows it on hookers and liquor, which I have seen happen a lot.  I have seen guys owe their whole check to other people from the number man to the liquor store where they have credit.

Weed had always been around long before I got there and it was no big deal.  When crack hit; it hit the plants hard.  It took some people to a whole new level.  GM had to deal with the same drug problems as other employers just on a much larger scale.  With drug programs to help all they could, to keep people coming to work.  Some people with drug problem did not come to work for a day or two after payday, starting soon as they got their check.

There were also some women out just to get a baby by a GM man, because when it came to child support GM doesn't play.  They just follow the court orders and take the money out like taxes. S some women treat it as the GM lottery for eighteen years.  I have seen men highly pissed, because of child support and anytime GM workers got bonus money it was hit by support payments first.  They got mad like it's not theirs.  They should not have to pay that much.

I bet the thought of having a baby never came into their mind when they were fucking. Now the support stays on their mind for eighteen years, and out of their checks like taxes.

Our boss was a short cowboy, named Dave with boots and all. On the first day at the team meeting he told us that he doesn't give a shit where we go and what we do as long as our job is covered. He was drinking from a coffee cup all the time. Not all coffee either; being about 5.2, it did not take much to fill him up and he was very easy to get along with. He wore shades and a cap all the time like Bert Reynolds in Smokey in the bandit; I know he had to see the movie to dress like that. It fit him too, right down to the bottle of liquor.

Now thinking back, I don't want to say he was not doing his job. He was drinking all the time. We were building side frames, which were mostly large pieces of sheet metal laid on a track line and welded together. As long as the side frames were welded by the robots when put in place it was all good. If he had been working in a department like trim or chassis he would have to keep a better eye on his people.

Most nights we were playing cards or at home, there was an open door policy and our boss knew we were there if our job done. He did not ask where we were; if he did not see you and the job was being done and your ass was covered.

We play card for hours, most time for cash. Drinking was done, undercover and out in the open in some of the break rooms. At the time, I would stop at Pete's liquor store, on the corner of Saginaw and Leigh Street. I would get my bottle of whatever I was drinking at the time and stop at KFC and get a large drink mostly ice. Fill my cup and sip all night on it.

One day I went over to Kert's job area during one of our breaks. One of his coworkers was sitting reading her bible, as I have seen her do many times before. I didn't know her name or anything about her. As we talked another guy named James came over. Everyone called him "Pimp" because he was always dressed clean, no matter what job he was on. He stood leaning against the stock basket. The lady got up and walked away about a minute after he got there. We all looked at her as she left. He said, "Y'all will not believe this shit that happen that night we went four hours last week." He said," that old girl there do a lot more than read the bible." (Nodding his head toward the ladies work station) He told us about his ride home after work with her.

I found out her name is Ms. P. He was telling us that she had been joking talking about the size of his feet. She wanted to know if his dick was anywhere near that size. He was surprised at her because she always had the bible in her lap ever chance she got. Pimp said to her that she will have to find out the hard way and gave her his pager no#. He said she wanted to ride in my new truck. She asked him to come over when the plant called four hours. He had gone to her house which was on south side of Flint off Lippincott, just pass the tracks.

He found the house and pulled up and blew the horn, she came out and hopped in and pulled away. He said, "As we got ready to make the right turn on to Lapeer Road she had leaned over and took out my dick and had it in her mouth." Kert and I are sitting in silence. As Pimp said, "as he drove he ran his hand over her ass and found out she had no panties on so he slid her dress up and started to play with her pussy." She continued to suck on him. He told us this went on until they got to Center Road. He said he was driving back to Lippincott, back to her house, and really gets busy. Kert and I are quite and listening hard.

He said, "I wasn't going to tell anybody but it was so fucked up I had to." anyway as he continued to tell the story his mood changed. He said, "Man just as we were coming up to Dort Road." She said, "Let me get comfortable." Pimp said, "She put her hands up to her mouth took out both sets of teeth and set them over the radio." We started to cracking up. He said, "That's not all." We listened. He told us that he forgot he was driving and could not take his eyes off the teeth. Until he felt the truck hit something. Pimp said, he looked up and was in the oncoming turn lane and had just ran a red light and jumped over the edge of the curb at Dort and Lippincott. We were now laughing our asses off. He was not finished. He said, as he tried to get the truck under control the teeth were sliding back and forth across the dash. He then told us, the lady had set up when he hit the curb and bounced back on the road. He said, she reached up and grabbed the teeth as they slid her way and snapped them right back in her mouth.

Pimp said he couldn't say one word. He just pulled in front of her house and said he had to go and that he was so mad that he almost crashed the truck when he ran a stop sign. Then he took a joint out of the ashtray that he was saving for later. When he put it up to his lips his nose got the smell of her pussy on his fingers. Pimp said he put the joint back down and started to smell his fingers.

He said whatever she had on smelled damn good. He had kept his finger up to his nose until he had gotten to his street then lit his joint. As Pimp is finishing, Ms. P comes back to sit at her station. We just sat there smiling. We had about five minutes before our break ended. I had to walk back to my job. As I passed her she flashed a big smile showing a very nice set of teeth and all I could do was smile back as I held back my laugh.

The strip club on Steward Street was remodeled and had some better-looking strippers, and changed the name to The Final Assembly. Anyone that worked at any GM plants got in free. They always seem to have a crowd, no matter what night. It was the only strip club in that area at the time, all others were way over on Dort highway. There was always someone outside trying to sell something. Hookers were always around. You only saw the cops if shit was wrong, and I know some of them were crooked. Some people just did shit as if it was legal, like playing the street lottery.

There were all kind of greasy spoon places around where you could call into from the plant and have lunch ready for pick up or they bring it to you at the gate. Anything from ribs to weed to having numbers played in the street instead of the store. It's been said that the union has had to step in when people running numbers have had problems over payouts, or lack of, and there was a numbers raid involving the police a few years later.

We had so much time sitting around that we had to think of shit to do just to stay awake sometime, and if sleepy, we took a nap. Or just tell somebody and go home. If they need you someone will cover you.

We also had people that played jokes all the time. One night, Flint had very bad thunderstorms, with tornado warning going off all over the plant. The plant was quiet except for the storm and most workers went to the safe areas in case the plant gets hit. Most of my team was just sitting in our break room playing cards, when we should have been in a safe area. One of our teammates climbed on top of the room and jumped up and down. Four of us were playing cards and one older lady was stretched out on her back on a table sleep, she looked dead but it was just the way she looked. She jumped up so fast she was just a blur and screamed as she was the first to make it to the door.

I never will know how she made it to the door before us. In a split second, we started knocking shit over trying to get out the door. The playing cards had been thrown in to the air. We knew the room had been hit by something big. Only to look up and see him laughing his ass off as we knocked each other over coming out the door. What was really funny was the old lady cussing him out for the next hour, and she was mad all night. But we should have been in a safe area anyway, that storm caused serious damage to a neighborhood near the plant on the other side of the river.

With only landline telephones at the time we could not go too far. Unless we knew someone was covering our job, just in case the line moved, which at this time were about 20 to thirty cars a day. There were days when I know lot of people did not come to work and got paid. This went on until we were up to about three hundred a day, at eleven and half hours a day.

The plant had too many extra people, because the plants used to make up Buick City had brought their people and Buick had called all their people back. There were people coming to work and all there was nothing for them to do but sweep. This really meant just get lost until they need you. Being on loan out to other departments that were short on people happened all the time; on Friday, just about all departments were short on people. Some people just did not come to work on Friday.

Kert and I still had lots of time off. Our job ran about ninety parts an hour and the line ran about fifty-five at the most. All we had to do was build up our parts and only one person in our group of five had to stay and feed them to the line. We would be done by eight or nine p.m. most nights and got paid till six a.m.

Sometimes if we did not have anything to do, I would let someone on the line go home. I could tell some were pissed that we were always gone from our jobs or just sitting around. We had learned all the jobs in our department, since we had so much time. We did feel a little guilty sometimes; not that much. This is about the time I started to read a lot, since I had a lot of time. I started with Donald Goings. I read all his books and anything else that held my interest. As time went own I must have read over 200 books while working on the line.

GM had a suggestion program where you suggest ways to do a job better that save the plant time or money. It was open to anybody that works there. If your suggestion was used, GM paid you according to the plant saving in time or money. Kert and I were having trouble with the trunk hinge staying in place, as it's screwed into the wheelhouse. We worked on a plan to get paid. We did not come up with shit. There were two skilled trade guys that worked on the welding equipment in the department. They asked if we could all work together and get paid. I quickly answered hell yea.

GM paid all names on the paper, if used. We told them we would let them know when we had a plan and they said the same. Kert and I were still blank about two weeks later when the skilled trades' guys showed us their plan and asked if we wanted to sign. We looked at the paper and look at the drawings and the descriptions of how it was to work. After asking a few questions, we signed the papers. We went to lunch not knowing what we just looked at, but did not want to look dumb either. Fuck it, if they get paid, we get paid.

The next week it showed up on the job and the skilled trades guys were there to show it. They wanted us to try the thing to see if GM would use it. Kert and I had already said that we do not give a shit if it work or not we using it just so GM would pay for the suggestion. It turned out to worked great and we all were paid.

It took BUICK CITY about ten months to go from twenty cars a day to five hundred and with all the extra people around rumors of layoff stayed in the air. We did not know when but we had been there long enough to know GM had to lay off some people soon. We were low seniority at the time so we knew we would be out for a minute. Just how long nobody knew. We just had to wait and see.

# "11. ROBBED BY THE COPS"

There were many places to get weed or anything else you want; any time of the day or night. Most folks that smoke know three or four places to get weed at any given time. If you trusted the young boys standing on the corner not to sell you grass they got from their front yard, you can hit them up sometimes.

One night at lunchtime, I left the plant to go to a house on Bishop St, right off King to get a dime bag. I had been there a few time before and you had to go around the back and knock on the window, when someone come just tell them what you want and they put it though a small hole after you pass the money through. I never met the person on the other side of the door so you never knew whom you are dealing with. You could find these houses all over the north side of Flint and you heard about them by word of mouth. You just had to know someone that had gotten some real weed there before, because you never knew what might come out of that hole where money go in first.

I parked in front of the house, and walked to the back, it was about 9pm and dark, I knocked on the window and the door opened, which was strange because that never happen before. There was a big black guy standing there, and he says, what you need? I told him a dime, and he says see that man right there, and pointed to someone further in the house. I had to step in to see who he meant. When I stepped in, he blocked the door behind me.

I look at the other guy; he was holding a police badge and smiling. Damn I say, he say ok grab some wall, I spread-eagle on the wall and got patted down. When I was allow to turn around there were about 6 cops there 2 in plain clothes, they asked for ID but it was in the car. There was another knock at the door and I was moved to front room. They were laughing and talking shit. They brought in another guy and after a pat down he was brought in with me. I heard someone say yawl need to hurry up. Another knock and I hear the door open and more voices, someone gets loud and I think he tried to run, the guy with the badge that had taken my 10 dollars came in with a clip board and asked us to write our names down. I wrote my name so shaky that a mail carrier can't read it, and then he opened the front door and said to get out.  I said can I get my 10 dollars back.  He did not say anything but by the look on his face, I could tell it was a lost cause.  As me and the other guy were walking out the door 2 more guys were heading to the back of the house, warning them never came to my mind I just wanted to get the hell out of there.

The whole thing took about 5 minutes and I was back at work pissed with no weed.  I looked in the paper the next few days to see if there was any news on the sting and never saw anything.  I never heard from the cops again; or my 10 dollars, but after thinking about it, straight cops would have at least given me an appearance ticket or something.  Not just taken my 10 dollars, and let me walk out the front door.  Who knows how many people went to that house that night.  It closed for about a week then they were back in business.  Nevertheless, I never went there again.  Being robbed is bad enough, but by cops really sucks.

# "12. SIX YEAR LAYOFF"

The layoffs came starting with low seniority first. Kert and I were in the first cut, after the temporary workers. We never knew how long a layoff was going last. However, as long as we were not off longer than we had work we had recall rights. We got unemployment and sub pay, which was about 80% of our pay.

Being off was ok at first, seemed like plants all over Flint had people off. GM had started to close some plants in Flint. At the time, I only thought we would be off for a few months at the most. I had offers to go to plants in New York, but I had no plans on going that far north. Flint was cold enough. GM had job-training programs and paid for school up to a certain amount. I was looking into taking classes in something.

The layoff turned from months to years. We just collected our pay thinking that we would be back before the money ran out. I took a class in bartending and truck driving and passed both. I couldn't stand the smell of liquor by this time. I could not find a job driving with less than two year's experience. I filled out job applications all over Flint, but no one was hiring laid off workers. They knew that as soon as GM called them back they would quit, and go back to GM. They would have to train someone else. Most ex GM workers were always looked over for jobs. Before I knew it the money had ran out and I found myself with no source of income. I was told by job search center to leave GM off my job applications that I filled out.

Unemployment with laid-off GM workers got very bad in Flint in the midst of the 80s and lots of workers lost their seniority and found other jobs. Michael Moore made a movie about Flint GM unemployment and how bad it got. I never saw the movie because I was there. I saw people getting put out of their home and on welfare. It was just a year or two before, they were on the line working, and doing well. Now seem like no one can find work to cover all the bills and no recall date in sight. I had been doing handyman work and anything else I could to get by until the callbacks started. I had always like working on cars and took a mechanic class that GM paid for. I was already what you might call a shade tree mechanic. There are many people that know how to fix cars. Unless you get papers showing what you know, you can never really get a job, as a mechanic. A mechanic helper or shade tree mechanic is all you will be in most states.

On the first day of class, the teacher told us that a mechanic would have the worse car on the road, because he will do just enough to keep it running; something about working on his own shit free. I got five state certifications in auto repair, and having that paper made the difference in working , because then people called me.

After getting my mechanic certifications, I looked for work at garages in Flint. I ended up doing more street mechanic work for people in my neighborhood. My first time having to use my mechanical knowledge was in court with a friend. He had taken his truck to a national chain garage, and it was still messing up. They would not even look at it again and he had given them $900.

When we got to court, he told the judge what the problem was. He told them I was a license mechanic, and that I had looked at the truck for him. I had told him the parts were rusty and looked used. He wanted the truck fixed with new parts or his money back. The judge never called me. He sent us in a room to talk it out. The garage offered to settle and as we went out the door, the garage manager pulled me to the side and offered me a job. I did not take it because they seem too shady and I might find myself in court with them again.

Before long, word got around that I fixed cars, house repair and clean up. I had people calling me all the time for just about anything. I had friends going with me as helping hands sometimes; or if I had a big job. I made mostly house calls like a doctor.

One day I got a call from an old man that I had did work for before. My friend Otis was with me. We had been best friends since the ninth grade. He had a sister in Flint, and had moved here the year before. When we got to the house over on Moore St, Mr. Jones met us on the front steps. He shook our hands and I could tell he was drunk or close. He gave me four one hundred dollar bills, and said that his car just stopped. He said it starts but won't move. I think the transmission is gone out he said. That's all I got until my check come and if it cost more let me know, I said," ok, let me look at it, and I will."

Otis and me walked over to the car and open the hood. I had him start it up and it sounded good. Then I had him put it in gear. There was lots of noise and the car didn't move. I look under the car and closed the hood, we walked back to the old man. I reach in my pocket and took the money out and gave him three hundred back. I told him he has a broken axel and $100 will cover it.

I could tell Otis had something on his mind by the way he was looking at me and looking up at the sky as if he saw a UFO. When we got in the car, he could not wait to clear his mind. He said, "We had $400 why you give it back?" We were both broke and I could see his point; as he kept talking about how dumb it was. I just looked at him. I said it would not cost $400 to fix that. "That old man don't know that," he said. "The money got to last him all month", I said. "He is only going to drink it up", he said.

"I do not give a shit what he does with it. I still wouldn't do it. He was still pissed but kept his mouth shut. I ended up dropping him off and fixing the car alone.

We did do all kinds of other small jobs together. One day a lady call me about putting a light up next to her carport on the side of the house. When we got there, she showed me the new light in a box. It was the kind that fit on a two-foot steel pole and come on at dark. She said it was like the one on the house that had went out weeks before.

We walked to the side of the house and looked up at the light. All we could see was the two-foot pole about twelve feet off the ground. The light was covered with bees. They had turned it into a beehive, but these were not honeybees. They were all over the light. Otis said, "Tell her she needs to call somebody to get them bees, and then we will change the light." I look at him and said, "She did call somebody. Us!"

He said, "Shit, I am not fucking with them bees." We stood looking at the bees. I told him that we can get the light with the bees still on it but we have to do it very slow. He laughed and said she can't pay enough to fuck with no bee's I said; we can put a big bag over the light. I went to get a ladder. I put it next to the light stirring up the bees a little. We waited for the bees to calm down. I got a clear forty-gallon garbage bag and some tools from the truck. We kept looking at the light until only a few bees were flying around. I opened the bag, told Otis that I was putting the bees in it.

He thought it was funny. As I climbed the ladder, I told him not to say a word that may upset the bees. "Don't worry," he said, because when they start to tear your ass up, I am going to be in the truck. I stepped up slowly trying not to be noticed. I was up to the bees and the light now; thinking this was a very bad idea. The bees sound like a big electric motor when thousands are three feet from your head. I turn and look down at Otis. He is in the truck looking up at me and pointing to a bee that is close to my ear. I just kept an eye on the bees that were flying around the light. The wind had been blowing just enough to keep the bag open. I turned sideways on the ladder and brought the bag very slowly over the light covering the bees.

I closed the bag around the pole and put a strip of tape around it. I had all the bees but about four or five, and they still seemed to be calm. I took the tools from my pocket, took the poll off the house, and cut the two wires. Handing it to him, who was out of the truck now, but still looking at the extra bees that had missed the bag.

I put the new light up. We packed up our stuff and got ready to go. I knocked on the door, told her we were finished. She asked, "How much she owed?" I told her, "$25." I gave Otis $10 and I kept $10 and put $5 in the gas tank. Gas was only about 80 cent a gallon back then.

By word of mouth, it got around that I was a good mechanic and handyman. I had calls coming from people all over Flint. I often had to find a helper just to keep up.

I did all kinds of work for all kinds of people. Every day I was hoping to be recall back to GM. I had been off for almost six years now and my time was running out. Anyone laid-off longer than worked, means they may lose all recall rights.

I took a class in truck driving in Cold water, Michigan, which GM paid for. This class is where you spent three weeks of training. I got a commercial driver's license (CDL) for truck driving. There were about twenty men in the class. At this time, unemployment in Michigan was very high. Most of the men in class had been out of work for a while.

The class cost about $3500 and it seems I was the only one with a check from GM, which paid for the whole class on the first day of class. The others were on some kind of work program from the state to put people back to work. We had to train 12 hours a day. There were some guys there that could not drive at all and did not even have a driver's license.

I had never driven anything bigger than a school bus and that had been years before. My first time behind the wheel was much easier than I thought it would be, after looking at some of the others stalled on takeoffs or grind too many gears. If you can drive a stick shift then you can drive a semi-truck. It was so easy my first time that they thought I had been driving before. I guess the school bus training kicked in. About half way through the class, we got a bad snowstorm. It snowed about two feet in about 12 hours. I had boots but not for this kind of shit. We still tried to train but the trucks became stuck all over the course. The boots I had on got soaked and seem to freeze on my feet. I ended up with frostbite and had to go to the hospital in Coldwater, Michigan.

My feet swollen and boots were excessively small now. When I was in hospital it seems that, everybody wanted to see my feet. Not sure if they never saw black feet or a black man. Everybody I saw was white and very nice. After giving me pain meds and wrapping my feet I was let go. The snow was getting worse and I was not about to be stuck in that town. I looked at my mummy feet and thought fuck it I am going home. I called and checked out of school and told them about the frostbite. They said to let them know when I would be able to come back. I packed and was on the road before dark. My feet were very sore and I could not get shoes on at all.

I drove as far as Lansing, Michigan and stopped for the night. The snow was still heavy but I had made it through the worse parts. I made it home the next day. By the time I unwrapped, my feet were all bloody and blisters were everywhere.

I ended up being out for about three weeks and went back. I passed all the tests. I got my CDL license. I tried to find a job driving. If you had at least two years over the road experience, you had no trouble getting a job. How you going to get two years and cannot get the job? They were not hiring unless you signed your name to a large contract to a company that got students jobs when they finished the class and got the CDL. I also got offers to drive cross-country for six cent a mile. The job would keep a driver on the road for weeks. I never drove a truck again.

GM had been in the news as they always were because they had been calling people back. I will just be glad when they get to my name. I got a letter from GM in 1992; it was an offer from GM to transfer to somewhere in Ohio. After getting the details, I took the offer and the paper work done. They had said they need 40 people and they were getting them from our area hiring pool. Days before I was to leave they called and cancelled, saying that they had to hire all the people in their area first and if they still need us they will let us know.

Anytime a plant need people the union did its best to guide its members to the open jobs anywhere in GM. I had turned downed an offer to go to New York. That was years ago and I would take that offer now. Before I go time for time, and they will not have to call me back.

# "13. THE FBI"

I have never been in trouble with the law; I avoid them as much as possible. I also try not to give them a reason to notice me. I was starting to think, we might never be call back to Buick. Finding work was getting harder. I found myself doing more and more street work.

In January on my birthday, I was working as a repairman for a local property owner doing simple things and clean up. I was sitting in the back office when two large white men in suits came into the rental office about eight that morning. I heard them say something to Mr. Turner, the old man at the front desk, in the office up front. He appears at the office door to tell Paula, the secretary, the men want to see her. They come in and show FBI I.D.'s in black wallets. I got up and head for the door; I have my work orders for the day. I need to get going before the snow started again. Just as I was about to go out the door, Paula calls me back in the office.

I went in and she introduced me. She thought maybe I was able to help them more than she could. I am thinking I don't know anything that the FBI needed to talk to me about. They shook my hand and took the two chairs that were by the window and pulled them up by the desk. I sat on edge of another desk against the other wall. They were asking about Benny. He used to work here but I had not seen him in weeks.

Paula asks me to tell them what I told her back in December, after looking at the news one day. At first, I was lost. I looked at her funny. Then one of the FBI guys said they were looking into a bank robbery in December. Then Paula said, "You remember when you called me that evening?

Then it hit me, I knew what she meant. I told the guys what I knew. Benny, The guy they were asking about was with me on the day of the robbery. This particular day, when I got home, the news was talking about a bank robbery in Saginaw about 5 pm that day. They showed a picture of the robber as he got away. I called Paula and told her that if Benny had not been with us all day, I would swear he was the robber. Saginaw was about 45 minutes away. I had left him at 4:15 p.m. to pick up my son. He was there when I left and, his car was not going to make it to Saginaw in that amount of time and get away.

Now Benny had been in and out of jail. If he had not been with me I would have bet money that he did it. He was trying to borrow $10 that day. However, he was always begging for money. He was a comic crack head that told jokes all day long. I have seen him jump in cop's cars joking and begging for a few dollars from them to get out. One cop even gave him $2 once to go fuck with cops in another car. I believe Benny was not very smart and the boss knew he would fuck up more than he worked. That was about half the people that worked here.

They started, to ask questions about him and that day in December. I told them about the whole day. They wanted to know everything but what I had for breakfast, which was nothing yet.

I remember that day well because the man I worked for had given me $100 to get a U-Haul truck and move a lot of toilets and sinks that were supposed to be in a house he just brought. We went to the house and there were about five toilets and a lot of junk.

Willie, my coworker and I got the toilets then we went back to office. I told the boss what we found. He looked up from his fish dinner and said, "I guess I brought a "pig in a coat"."

He said, "Well go out back, get that pile of shit, and take it to the dump." I said, "You mean the big pile of trash in the alley?" He said, "Yes!" I said, "You cannot put that kind of shit in that truck". He turns and asked Mr. Turner, "When you rent them big ass trucks can't you haul what you want?" "Yep", Mr. Turner said, "long as you clean it out". Boss looks back at me and said, "Go move that shit."

It was at that time I told the FBI that Benny had showed up in the alley and offered to help. Sometimes I give guys a few dollars to help on dirty jobs. It was cold and he had no gloves. He was begging for $10. I didn't give it to him. He and his friend went in and out of one of the apt that was being painted.

They were there most of the day that we could see and when we took the truck back. It was after 3:30 p.m. and they were there when I got back at 4pm. When I left, to get my son he was in the office joking with Paula at about 4:15p.m.

If the FBI has ever questioned you, it is not like being question by the cops. They questioned you looking for lies. They asked the same questions 4 or 5 times during questioning in a different form trying to trip you up. They looked at your every body movement as you answer and how long it take to answer. In addition, they write everything down and kept looking at it as if they missed something.

While, they were questioning us; which must have being going into the two hours, the phone ranged. It was Benny, he talked to Paula. She pulled out a book, said, "Ok I will tell them". After looking through the book for about a minute; then she hung up the phone.

At this time, we were still kind of in the dark and they had just been asking questions. They asked me if I was sure about the date, he was there. I said," Is that the first day it was on the news?" He said, "Yes!" Then, I said, *Yes"

It turned out that I was not the only one that saw it, and said it looked like Benny. He had been arrested and charged with the robbery. His phone call was to tell Paula that that was the day that his girlfriend moved to the apartment by the office. He was helping her move and fucking with us as we loaded the big U-Haul. She looked in the book and showed the FBI the calendar

He was right, he was there that day but had wittiness that can put him about 50 miles from the bank at the time of the robbery. They asked a few more questions before they pulled the photos from the robbery taken in the bank. They put them on the table; as we looked, we were speechless. It was Benny all the way down to the thick black frame glasses with tape holding one handle on, to the big silver ring he wore with a faded initial on it. It was all clear in the pictures from different angles.

We slowly said, "That's Benny". However, he was here. I know he was here, when I left that day, I took a good look at all three pictures. I could only say that it was Benny in the pictures, along with Paula. They thanked us, packed all their shit, and looked over the notes they had written. Just before they went out the door, one turned and asked Paula about Benny's girlfriend. She said, "She had only stayed a month and had moved just last week." they told us, "goodbye." They got into their dark sedan and drove away.

After they were gone, we talked about that day. Benny would have had to be flying to make it to that bank that far away. We just said, "Well he just back in jail." it was nothing new to him. After looking at pictures, we thought he did it. The FBI pictures were stronger than our words.

We forgot about him until another bank robber had been caught a few months later. He could have been Benny's twin, right down to the ring and eyeglasses. The Flint Journal ran a story on it. They had both pictures on the front page and it was like a mirror image.

I ran into Benny a few months later, he had been let go. He said he was picked up because someone saw the picture on the news the day after the robbery. He was let out after five month and they were trying to offer him $100.00 for the mistake. He was beaten and his hearing was fucked up now. He wanted a million. He was looking better than I had ever seen him in a long time and had picked up a little weight. Jail seems to have done him good compared to the last time I had seen him. Maybe, he should pay them. The last time I saw him was the only time he did not hit on me for cash. I just hoping GM call me back soon. "

# "14. BACK AT BUICK"

In 1993, after being laid off for six years Kert and I were called back to a plant in Saginaw Michigan, about 40 minutes north of Flint on I 75, where GM made steering columns for GM vehicles and other car companies. They ship them all over the world. Working there was cool; I was given a fork truck along with two other men that were in the group. I had never driven a fork truck but I was not telling them that, I ask how I got that job, and he said it was in my file that I had fork truck training.

Thinking back to when I was hired; a few new hires, and me were sitting at a lunch table with a union rep, and someone asked about truck driving jobs. He opens up his bag and gave us all a form to fill out about fork truck. I guess that was my training.

They gave me a fork truck and sent me out back to practice for about half the shift on empty tubs and racks in the back of the plant. I did ok the first hour but by the fourth hour I had it down and was ready for some real heavy shit, or so I thought. It is a big difference in empty crates and picking up three or four at a time filled with steering columns.

It took a little getting used to driving backwards down the aisle when loaded. I loaded trucks, and had to supply parts to the line in my area. The job offered lots of Saturday overtime. Kert was on the line not too far away. He was not crazy about being there but he was working with some pretty women. Work was good until July changeover, which is when GM shutdown for two week to switch over to the next model year.

We were laid off again, and call right back after 2 weeks, he went back to the steering gear plant and I went to another plant in Saginaw across the river. It was the worse plant I ever been in. It was where they did heat treatment; hot ovens were everywhere oil was all over the floor and on anything else you touched. I was on third shift and it was always hot. This was not a place to wear good clothing if you wanted to keep them. I had to take the parts out of whatever oven I was watching and pack them in crates to be shipped out. I still managed to get two or three hours sleep a night, because it took hours for the parts to roll out and I had to wait until the parts came to me. I got off at 7 am and still had to drive back to Flint.

We had heard that Buick was calling people back home, and had been hoping to be back before winter. The call came the next week and our 45-minute drive to work turned to 10 minutes. This time was different, the plant was running like a clock and everyone was working. We were pumping out about 550 to 600 cars a day doing 9 hours. We were in different parts of the plant but still saw each other at the liquor store parking lot tree, it was a big tree in the parking lot behind the liquor store, on North Street off Leith, a GM worker hangout spot. If anybody was working there would be someone under that tree taking a break or selling something.

Buick having so many plants, working difference shifts there was always someone working somewhere. I moved from dept. to dept., doing all kinds of line work and repairs. Being a mechanic already gave me an edge on learning jobs. Sometime you had 3 days to learn a job, but I never took that long. I was loaned out a lot when I first got there because I didn't have a job assigned to me. I did repair jobs where the Forman gave me a number and told me to find the car wherever it was in the plant and repair whatever is wrong with it.

I love doing thing like that so I could fuck off an hour or so, it only took minutes to fix the repair whatever was. If I was gone too long the Forman let me know I should have been back. I just tell him that the car was in the overhead bank and I had to wait on it.

I had lots of free time if I was not on the line and was in and out of my area all over the plant. No one knew me when I was out of my area, so I had free run of the plant until the wrong person came to like me, but it was cool.

One day the plant manager came in with two other guys in suit and ties. He came and talked to my boss at the time Dick. He needs some extra people somewhere. I was sitting reading the newspaper when my boss called me over. I knew who he was and had not seen him in a long time. He shook my hand and asked how I was. My boss said, I was a fast learner and he didn't need me right now.

As I shook his hand I said, I heard you been sick, he said yea I had a heart attack and had to have a pacemaker. O yea I said, well Dick told us you ate a bad piece of pussy. Dick's eyes got big and he look as if I had just called his mother a whore. Nobody said anything; I bet he was thinking how dare I say that to his boss.

Then the plant manager started to laugh. He laughed so hard I thought he was having another heart attack. By this time all the men were laughing and Dick had gotten the color back in his face. I had been careful to make sure no women were close enough to hear me. Talk like that around women can be big trouble if reported. I looked at Dick and he was looking at me as if we just dodged a bullet, he said to go with him and stay as long as he needs you.

The plant manager was still kind of laughing with the other guys as we walked to the back of the plant making small talk. He took me to the dept. where they needed me. As I met the trainer in that dept., the plant manager was talking to the Forman, and as I walked by, I heard him say bad piece of pussy and they both started to laugh.

I was not able to walk around like before because; he knew who I was and where I belonged. Anytime he saw me after that he always took time to speak or chat. About two months later Dick asked if I wanted to become a Foreman. I was not ready for that, so I passed. Foremen were always getting yelled at and not in the union. He asked again the next month. However, I was happy doing what I was doing and I am sure I would not be happy in a tie every day.

Later that year I went to a department in final assembly where I drove the new cars off the end of the line. It was a dream job. I knew it would not last long because there were too many old people working around me. Which meant it was a high seniority area. I had about 13 years now and that was not enough time to be working that easy. There is nothing like being the first one to drive a new car off the end of a GM assembly line. After the first few hours of getting in and out of new cars I was kind of wishing the people can come and get they own damn cars.

Working overtime in that department was off the hook. Any over time was driving new cars around the plant. We had three or four different brands of cars to move, one was the 96 OLDS SS Bonneville, and it was one of GMs fastest cars at the plant. We always jumped at the chance to drive one because of the takeoff it had.

There was a long narrow strip behind the plant leading to a big lot where new cars were stored. We used to go as fast as we could and make a sharp turn.  If anybody hit the wall, you were out.  The fastest you could go was about 35 and make it; if you were good.  If you hit the wall, just park the car and walk away.  I never saw the wall hit, but I saw the cars that hit it.

I knew I would not be there long, it was too easy.  I was sent to the body shop again.  I started working on a line where I had to hold a big ass spot-welder and hit about six spots on the body of the car as it came down the line.

Later I hooked up with a group where doors were put on.  Right away, we were back to doublings up with 2-1/2 hours on and 2-1/2 off. Doubling –up was not for all jobs.  It had to be a job where both could work with no sweat and you had to trust that the other person was good enough to do both jobs.  If anything went wrong, you both may be in trouble.  I was loaned out once to a dept. where 4 guys were doubling up and, one got to take a day off every week and got paid as if he were there.

Not all plants were so laid back; some had gates where you had to clock out to leave the plant anytime you wanted to leave.  There were guards at most plants main gates, some have a turnstile.  Sometime during the working hours at some plants you had to have a paper signed by the supervisor to get out the gate.  Buick was the only open gate plant I was ever in and people took full advantage of it for years.  With all the bars and clubs around the plant it seem like everybody that went in and out  during working hours drank or did some kind of drugs.

The one thing most workers hate is when we been at work all day and overtime is called at the last minute, like 4 of 5 more cars will make a difference.  I was just so glad to be back at work.  Being off six years had been a long time to be laid off.  If it had not been for God and street work I don't think I would have made it with no one in a rush to hire laid off GM workers.

# "15. DEATH AT WORK"

Around Christmas time in the middle of the 90s, we had about 3 days before the break. There were parties all over the plant all week long. A lot of folks were drinking and some people don't come back from lunch if they have too much fun. The bars and the other clubs were jumping and snow was about 6" thick. A few people that didn't party or drink or anything just stayed at their work station.

I was working on line about 7pm near the front door by the body shop when word came that two men had gotten hurt. It was just after break, when we heard that one man was dead. Nobody knew for sure what was going on, but we could see blue lights though the doors and the fire trucks.

We were getting bits and pieces of what was going on; it was not good at all. The line where I was never stopped, so we had to get news in bits and pieces as it came from the people who were back there in the body shop where it happened. That whole area was shut down; a lot of the folks went home from that department.

Later one of my friend that was there came and told us what had happen, he said the guys had to set a die press in place, now a die press is a big block of steel that fall on a sheet of steel and press it into hoods, trunks, doors, or whatever they making at the time

He says it looked like they missed taking loose one of the hooks before they lifted the hoist. The one hook was not strong enough to hold the die press and it flip out pinning them to the floor. The thing was so heavy that he says there was nothing no one could do, the men yelled, and screamed and people tried to help but the die was too heavy to move, even with a fork truck, only way to move it was with the crane that dropped it.

He say that one man was trapped at the waist down and the other at the hip, and they had been smashed to about 1 inch thick, both men yelled at first then one just looked around and died all within about 3 minutes of getting trapped. They had to cut the other man leg off and rush him to Hurley hospital.

The guy that died was moved from the plant somewhere in the am. His family had been brought to the plant after finding out about his death. It was also his last day to work. When I got home, the news said him and his family were planning on going south to spend the holidays with kin in Mississippi when he got home from work.

It was later said that both had been drinking and not supposes to be doing the job they were on. The whole thing was unreal. It put a big damper on the plant for the rest of the year

There are so many safety meetings that something like this should never have happen. I know that GM puts the safety of its workers first and always have. The biggest danger we have is fork trucks, you have to look both ways like you do in the streets, and make eye contact with driver if truck is close to you.

In January, when we came back to work, I was walking in the body shop and came across one big press that had yellow caution tape all over it. It hit me that this was the place where the accident happen.

I got a cold chill and never went to that area again. I don't think they ever used that press again. People get hurt all the time and depending on the injuries or accident a drug test will follow.

# "16. DRIVE BY SHOOTING"

We were on a week layoff in February of 1994. We were always off three or four weeks a year for something that is unplanned. I was ready for the well-needed rest. We were on nine hours shift and cars were selling like crack. Due to a parts shortage, we would be down a week.

The week went bad that Sunday night with a call that some kinfolk had been shot, and was at the hospital. I ended up at the hospital most of the night. After getting to the hospital and finding a few family members already there. I found out it was his ex that shot him. She took him to ER, dropped him off and went to park the car. I saw cops talking to her and I saw her daughter. I asked, what happened?

All she said, "Momma shot him." I turned to look at her mom. She was in the back of a police car. Then I turn and went in to find the rest of my family to see how he was.

The doctor came in after about an hour or so and told us he was fine for now. He had been shot twice in the stomach and lost a lot of blood. He was stable for now. The waiting and the stress of not knowing had been tearing us up. When something like this happen the behind the scene stress on the family is unbearable. You reach for any news you can get on your love ones. Now that we had some news I was tired and wanted to get to bed, so I headed home. I had the week off from the plant. I went back to bed soon as I got home. Being at the hospital all night was worse than being at work.

Awakened by the phone ringing, I sat up to answer it. At first, I didn't hear anything then I heard kids laughing and the phone went dead. I hung up and lay back down and about ten minutes later, it rang again. "Hello", I said. "Yo momma!" I heard in a kid's voice. "What," I yelled, "who is this?" The phone went dead again. This was in 1994 before caller ID. So all I could do was just hang up.

I got about seven more calls that morning before 8am. It was all-quiet and I fell asleep again. The phone woke me again around noon it was my family calling to say he had pulled though. He would be in the hospital for a while and filled me in on the latest details of the shooting.

As I was taking a shower, I heard the phone again. I hopped out to get it and almost fell. I was thinking it may be more news from the hospital. When I picked it up somebody said, "Hi bitch" "What?" I said. They said, "You heard me." In the background, I could hear kids laughing their asses off. The phone went dead. I thought if I cussed them out and let them know I am grown. I don't play kid games hopefully the calls would stop. I tried that a lot.

This went on for about three days. I was getting calls before these kids went to school and soon as they came in. I guess they had been going through the phone book fucking with folks. I guess I was their target for the week. I talked to kids from the ages of 6 to 16 boys and girls. They would just call all night long. I could not leave phone off hook because of kin in hospital. One day when the little boy called me to cuss me out for about the 10th time that day. I heard his mom,

"Yell who you talking to." She took the phone from him and she said, "Hello."

"Hi, Miss," I said, "can you please stop your kids from calling me they been doing it for four days now." Click, the phone went dead. Damn, I thought now I know where they get it. I did notice that the phone did not ring for hours. So I am thinking maybe she did fix it. About 15 minutes later the ringing started again this time it was worse. The mom must have said something to them because it got so bad. I called the operator to report them and all I was told was that I could change my number and that would take two business days. Being Thursday it would be

Tuesday before the number would change. They don't count Saturday and Sunday. So I told her to go ahead and change it.

As I was on the phone the kids were beeping in on the other line. I told her. She said there was nothing she could do. All I had to do was wait until Tuesday and it would be all over. I wanted to see if I could find the house before Tuesday from the young boy. I knew the calls would come until then. The 6-year-old boy called later that day and I got him to talking about his age, which was 6, and he had two brothers and a sister he did not know their age but said they were all older than him. I asked him where he stayed and he got quiet. I thought he hung up but then he said on North St by Pierson Road that was about 5 minutes away. It was a long one-way street near the plant. Somebody came into the room and he hung up. I got in my car and went over to North Street not knowing who I was looking for but I had a good idea.

Nothing on North Street caught my eye. But as I crossed Pierson Road going past Marengo Street, one big blue house stood out in the middle of the block off North St. I parked and watched the house for about five minutes.

Kids were going in and out of the house. From looking at the house and the junk car in the driveway, I don't think they were the kind of people that you can knock on their door and say they kids fucking with you. I just drove by the house and looked though the picture window to see kids jumping on the bed. I had found the house. I just had to make sure this was it. I went home and checked my answering machine, which I had just gotten to screen my calls and the kids filled both sides of the tape with all kinds of shit and prank calls.

I knew the calls would come. They always do and it did not take long, it was the 6 year old, just as I hoped he called the most. I guess he thought we were friends. I told him, "I knew where he lives." he said, "no I don't," I said, "on the corner of North and Marengo" he said, "I don't live on the corner." I said," you live in the big blue house right?"

He said, "Yea!" then I said, "If they don't stop calling me I will come tell your mom." he hung up. About a minute later the phone rang again it was the oldest old and she was mad. I told her I had their address. I told her what it was to let her know I was for real. She cussed me out and said, "Come on!" Then she hung up the phone. The calls kept coming for the rest of the evening and I knew what I had to do. I don't give a damn if they are kids I was fed up.

I had always been a good shot, now it was time to test my skills. I went to Kmart on Pierson Rd with one thing in mind getting those kids. I went right to the sporting goods department and found the weapon that I needed. After paying for it and looking at the time, I had about 2 hours before it would be dark enough to do what I had in mind.

The time was here. I got my lady to drive my van. I opened the sunroof. We rode past the house so I could show her which one. I got in the back, so I could stand up in the roof. We went down two blocks so we would not have to turn on North Street. We set at the stop sign looking at the house for about a minute. I told her to just go like normal and that I would get only one shot.

Now I am not stupid I would never shoot into a house full of kids with a gun of any kind no matter how many times they called. I will use a slingshot, not just any slingshot, but a wrist rocket. I had been shooting slingshots all my life. My brothers and I used to make them out old coat hangers or a strong tree branch. A shot like I needed to make a homemade one won't cut it. I needed the real thing.

It is a slingshot that's used to hunt and I was using a tire lug I had gotten from the plant as ammo." "

We were right in front of the house and it was all dark now except the room upstairs, where I saw kids jumping on the bed. " "

The big picture window at the front porch was my target. As we drove by, I was standing in the sunroof with the slingshot ready and all I had to do was draw back aim and shoot. I took aim and hit the top center of the glass expecting all hell to break loose with the breaking of glass. Nothing happened. The lug went through the glass and made a hole the size of the lug nut and knocked the curtain back. Not one sound was heard, as she drove away. " "

I went home and waited for the cops to come, I had both sides of the tape from the answering machine if needed. They never did show up. I guess the kids never told whom they think did it and why. Then they would have had to tell why I was after them. The calls stopped. Until one Sunday night and I laughed and asked, "How they like the window?" She cussed me out. I said, "I will be back since you want some more." "    "

Monday at work, I was telling Kert about it. I wanted to take out that big window and another shot would do it. At first break, we drove by the house. There was a big X made with black tape across the hole in the window where I had shot it. We talked and I decided to do it at lunch when it would be dark." "

At lunchtime, Kert and a lady friend, got in my van and drove by the house. We drove around the block. Kert asked, "If I wanted to wait till we got off since house was lit up." I did not see anybody outside and I don't give a shit if they up or not. Let's do it now. I got in place and got the slingshot ready. He drove normal down the street.  I took the shot and missed, I hit the door frame and it sounded like a shotgun.

Kert took off as if we were being shot at.  My body lifted off the floor of the van as we shot down the street.  I almost dropped my slingshot before I could drop back down in the van.  We made it to the corner of Saginaw Street and made a right and went to Pierson Road and made another right back on North Street.  We passed the house on Marengo Street.  We looked and saw house was dark and the cops were there.  It had only been about two minutes.  I don't know how in the hell they got there so fast.  Anyway, we just went back to the tree in the liquor store parking lot and finished our break. I never heard from the kids again.

# "17. MOVING TO TENNESSEE"

In 96, I was working in the body shop. I had spent a week in a class that the union had offered. About 25 workers got to spend a week at an off sight location. We went to a hotel in Flushing Township, where the union had rented a meeting room. We were to be paid just as if we were at work.

We only had to be in class 8 hours, but were being paid whatever our line was running, and we were on nine hours. We talked about the start of the union and the plans for the future. We got to ask any questions we had.

There we different union reps come in and talk to us on whatever office they held. They told us how the foreign car companies were building cars at a lower cost than GM, and if things don't change they would take over. At the pace they were going, it won't be long.

On the last day of class the union president came in, as he talked to us, he said that Buick City had no contract from GM to build cars past 1999, and if they did not get one Buick City would close.

I had not thought about leaving Flint, but if the plant closed, I may have no choice. I did not want to go through that long layoff shit again. That was about three years away, and if the plant was closing by 1999 is would be phasing some departments out soon.

GM had been moving people around to open jobs in others states if they wanted to go. I got to thinking that it might be better to look for a new plant somewhere soon before word got out about the plant closing. In the next 12 months I kept, checking to see what plants needed people from a list in the personal office.

The only place I really wanted to go to was Saturn in Tennessee. I had put in to go there before. Saturn was very meticulous about whom they hired, and I was not called, but I did get a free trip. In 1989, Saturn had flown my girl and me down for an interview for 3 days. They paid, for everyone to come down, and be interviewed for a few days. We also toured the town and the plant, which was still being built.

After flying us down and spending all that time there, I got the letter that I was not what they were looking for. To this day, I do not know what they were looking for. We were all line workers and they seem to think they were getting the best of the best. On the other hand, were trying too. It was supposed to be a new kind of Car Company. The one thing I noticed when there is that the plant was way off the highway. There were no beer and wine or liquor stores anywhere near it. It seems to be in the middle of a hay field, and a big ass barn in front of the plant.

I decided to put in to go back to Saturn and see what happen. I had a friend there and called to see what she could do. I guess in the 8 years since I first tried they lowered their standards.

They called me for another interview and this time they just flew me down and gave me a rental car. On the last day of the interview, two women I had met were hoping that the bus got them back to the airport by 6pm so they could get on an earlier flight.

I told them I am not on the bus, and that Saturn had gotten me a rental car. One asked how I got a car and no one else did. I say shit, I thought everybody got one. She says, well we all going to airport and we going with you.

We made it to the airport and got on the plane. We were all from flint. Flying into Detroit then driving to Flint a storm set in as we sat on the runway waiting to takeoff. We had all taken seats in the back of the plane in a three-row section. As I look out the window I said, damn if we crash we are going to get wet. The woman next to me said, yes, that rain is coming down. Then she realized what I said and kinda rolled her eyes.

I noticed the other woman had not said a word since getting on the plane and seem to be praying. Her friend said that it was her first time flying. I said you never flew before? She shook her head no. Have you ever been out of Flint? I asked. Yes, she said, then closed her eyes and went back to praying to herself. As the plant took off everything was going good and she was still praying until the planes landing gear went up. When the wheels went in and the doors closed, we must have been sitting right over that area because there was a big bump on the floor under our feet. She jumped up, and screams O Jesus! Loudly it caught me and the other lady by surprise.

We looked up and all the people up front were looking back at us. For the rest of the trip, everything was funny as me and the other lady looked at her friend trying to keep it together. It was funny but I was a little scared when we went through the storm and the plane was shaking a lot.

About 2 weeks later, I got the call that; I had been accepted and had about a thirty-day window to get there by Easter weekend in 1997. I was all packed and ready to move to Tennessee. Working at Saturn was different than any plant I ever been. The rules were different but the work was the same. The lines still snake though the plant and workers work side by side to build the best car they can.

People toured the plant on trolley trains and watched us as we worked. Saturn gave one of the biggest owner parties I ever saw. A weeklong of plant tours, cars shows, and music. From what I was told the SATURN HOMECOMING cost around 10 million dollars for the week. It was worth it all if true. It was just hard getting used to the small town where the cow pasture is next to the mall and everything closed at dark.

They had a holiday called mule day in Columbia, Tennessee, where mules from all over the county came to town for a parade. I was not too amused and could care less about the parade because from what I was told by one of the locals that they been doing this over 100 yrs and back then black people were sold along with the mules. The black people seem to have their own celebration going on later at night partying on about 3 blocks strip with food, music and anything else you wanted.

I don't think the people in the town like the people that transferred in, some felt that the jobs should go to the locals. It was here I did very little street work. I picked up weight and went to over 200 pounds for the first time in my life. The work was the same at any other plant except, we did job rotation in most departments where you switched jobs every hour. We were working under different rules, if we had a different way of doing things all we had to do was see if all agreed with it and it worked with other teams, then it was voted in.

It was the 1st plant where I worked that you had to drive down a long road to the plant with fields on both sides of the road, working here seems to be the place to be. They have good bonuses every quarter of the year, but it was still a GM plant. The work was the same everywhere.

This was the first plant where the worker had a say in the day to day running of the plant and the parts we used. We had a checkup system where we could contact other departments if we saw something they missed or needed to do, we just call them and they sent someone over to take care of it. We also could contact the supplier of our parts if we were having problems with them.

I remember when we painted the fence at Saturn. It was hot that day and there were hundreds of team workers scraping and painting the fence. Each with a section to do like we do on the line. The world may have seen the commercials but we did the work. It was not just for show.

Saturn also allowed us to go to other plants and see how they worked, when we had some time off. At the time it seems like the plant would be there for years, now just less than 15 years later it sit idle. I am not sure what they will build, but in my opinion if the plant closes forever the after effect will be far worse than in Flint, Michigan in the long run for the town. The workers will be ok. GM transferred them in and they can transfer them out. All the homes they leave vacant will be hard to sell, and some stores will not have enough customers to stay open. Also after the workers money run out if he doesn't follow GM or take a buyout he may lose everything; including their spouses. I hope and pray for them to be up and running soon.

# "18. HIGH-SPEED POLICE CHASE"

Whenever anyone get hired at Saturn, back then everybody had to spend the first 2 weeks in a class learning about the town and the plant. The class was very informative, it told how the plant came about, and showed video of the plant being built; they told us what they expect from us and what we can expect.

We went over the plant rules and filled out all kinds of employee forms. The class had about 20 people in it, about half and half of men and women; but just one that I will never forget. Her name was Rita Bass, and she was fine, the kind of woman that wake up looking good. She was about 26 and had just finished college and Saturn hired her to work in Northlake the corporate office at Saturn

At the end of the 1st week, we had gotten to know each other good after being in class 8 hours a day. Rita was very cool and down to earth, but was all business, and even took notes in class. She reminded me of Jasmine Guy a little. With long hair and not that shit from a horse ass and a very nice shape but she only wore business suits to class.

Friday I was sitting with Kenny, a foreman that came to be a supervisor from Ohio. He lived in the same apartments as I did. We wanted to hang out in Nashville that night, but did not know the town or where to go. Rita lived there so we asked her about some places to check out. We were thrilled when she accepted our offer to join us.

That night Kenny and I drove to Nashville and were to meet her at the club. We got there, parked across the street, and waited for her. We saw her pulling in and walked over to meet her. As she got out Kenny and I said, damn at the same time. She was dressed nothing like at work. She had on jeans that look like she was poured into them and I am not sure what color top I only remember the jeans.

We walked back across the street to the clubs. Which had bars and clubs on both sides and lots of people were out. She was walking between the two of us and people were looking at her. She was not the kind of woman I would have gone after too. Not because she look so sexy but by looking at her nothing I ever saw her in was cheap. In addition, my pockets were not that deep. Therefore, I was very glad just to be hanging out with her. We went in a club called Mural Bulls; it was a little slow and ritzy for us. It was nice, and she asked if we want to go to a club called Club Yesterdays in the hood.

Kenny let her drive his car since she lived there and knew where we were going. We got in and as we went through downtown Nashville she showed us some landmarks, I don't remember what they were, but she was pointing and talking.

About 10 minutes into the ride we pulled up to a red light and stopped, she looked in the rearview mirror and yelled; O shit! She started to pull off. Another car was going through the light and she slammed on the brakes. Just as she was about to say something the car was hit hard from the back and it knocked us about 10 feet under the light. As we looked back to see what hit us, we saw a white van.

We started to get out and check the damage when the van made a U-turn and took off the other way. Rita looked at Kenny and, Kenny yelled get him; she gunned the caddy and did a donut and was on his ass in about 3 seconds. I was in the back seat looking from the center of the seat when I could. We were weaving all over the road and I was being bounced from side to side as she passed anything in front of her.

I remember seeing a police officer at a car he had stopped, not sure if he was just stopping them or was just letting them go. We were in a curve and I saw him look at the van fly by then he looks at the caddy right on his ass. He was running to his car when I looked out the back window, and soon he would be just one of many cops' cars to join the chase. At first I thought cool, now that the police here, this fool will stop. No such luck, we were picking up speed and fast. I was looking from side to side and back to front. Looking out the back window, I saw that there were about three police cars now. In addition, I saw a few more at some intersections that we passed through, they must have called and had traffic blocked. Now we were off the main highway and starting to go through neighborhoods.

I have no idea how many cops were in the parade now but the inside of the caddy was blue from the lights, and cops had bright ass spotlight on us most of the time. Rita stayed on his ass. He made a few sharp turns and so did we; it was at that time I got to see about how many police cars were in the chase. I did not even try to count them, I just remember looking down the block and the line went from one end to the other. They were still coming when we made another sharp turn; this went on for what seem like forever.

We were not doing much talking, we just yell if we had a narrow escape, of which there were many. Rita drove as if she had done this before. She had that mad black woman look on her face, not saying a word, just looking at the van. She was driving as if she was in a NASCAR race, trying to win a big race, without the helmet. At this point, I was scared as hell and the police were not making it any better. I could tell she was not stopping, cops or not, so I just kept looking and holding on.

We made a turn on a one-way street with cars parked on both sides. About ¼ ways down the block the van stopped behind a parked car on the right side of the street. Rita stopped in the middle of the street blocking the van from taking off again. We all jumped out of the caddy at the same time and ran around to tell the cops what happen. The cops did not want to hear anything, all we saw and heard was get your hands up, there were so many people yelling to get on the ground, or get your hand up they all had nine mill pistols pointed at us. We were yelling that he hit us! He hit us! And they were yelling just as loud.

As we tried to get our hands up and explain about the van, they were steps away from getting close enough to get hands on us and take us down, when the van driver's door popped open. Everybody froze, and stop yelling at the same time, we all looked at the van. A little old white man fell out across the back of the caddy and slid to the ground. Two of the cops went and caught his arms and helped him up, he was drunk as a skunk, and had a cut on his hands from breaking his bottle and a cut on his head. He had no tags, no driver license, or insurance and just got the van that week; he was about 60 and seems to have done the DUI thing before. As the cops put him in handcuff, he told them he had lost his license to drinking a long time ago and just drove to and from work.

Within minutes, the street was filled with fire trucks and medics. The police had guided us down a one way street where we never would have made it to the other end. There was no room to pass so the van had to stop; the police cars were blocking the street waiting at the other end.

As we were starting to get our nerves back one of the cops said, Rita is that you? She says yea and he burst out laughing. It turns out that she work with the city council and knew most of the cops there. She had their attention now more than when they had guns pointed at our heads thinking we had jacked the caddy. Seem like all the cops there came to chat with her and make sure she was ok. I think they came to get a better look at her in them jeans. They never asked if we were ok, and that's cool long as they had put the guns up.

We finished the reports and she asked, if we still wanted to go to the club. After looking at the car and finding just a broken taillight and a small dent in bumper. It was about 11:30 by now; she said the club was not for away. We headed that way and went and had a good time. We stood out like cops at the club; Tony and I were dressed in plain slacks and shirts.

There were gold teeth, pagers on most of the men and some had long Geri curls, and some even had two pagers and made sure they were where they could be seen. I saw more fake ponytails on women than at a farm and woman in shit they should not put on even if they got it in their size; let alone 3 sizes too small. Before we got there Rita had told us not to tell any of the women there where we worked at. Now I see why, they all seem to be out to catch and the men seem to be showing off.

Kenny and I sat at a table Rita had led us too; she went walking around. We saw her talking to people all over the club. It seem like she knew everybody.

Looking at her it is not hard to be her friend. She came and sit with us and ask why we not dancing. I do not dance and will look stupid trying to dance with her. We talked and she told us about the club and some of the people there, a slow song came and I asked her if she wanted to dance. She looked at me and said, don't even try it and pointed at some women standing by the bar and said, I brought yawl here to have a good time with them not with me. Kenny danced with a few women but I just sat at the table taking to some girl Rita had left there before she wondered off again.

The Monday in class the three of us could not look at each other with a straight face before someone would break out laughing sometimes disturbing the class. At first break, we told the class about the wild Friday night we had.  The end of class that week was the last time I saw her for about a year then saw her at a Saturn function. My team leader and I were there and I pointed Rita out and asked if she remembered the car chase I had told her about my first week here.  She said yes and I said well she was driving.  She said you lying, I say nope and we walk over to Rita.  When she finishes talking to two older white guys she turns and sees me and started to laugh as she gives me a hug.

My team leader says she never met her but heard there was a very pretty black woman at Northlake that was smart.  Saturn had snatched her right out of college.  Then she looks and says what the fuck she doing out with you? She was just showing us the town I said.

# "19. MOVING TO ATLANTA"

When I got to Saturn in 1997, I thought it would be there forever. I had to quit GM to go there because they were not supposed to be a part of GM. Things changed and in just two years I was on the move again. This time it was to the Doraville van plant; right outside Atlanta, Georgia. Moving to Atlanta from Tennessee was kind of like when I moved from Arkansas to Michigan."

"They were only taking about forty people. You needed twenty years of seniority to go. That is just what I had at that time. At the meeting, it did not take them long to make up their mind. I was on my way. The window to move was only two weeks. I had to be there September 1999."

"Traffic in Atlanta was no joke. There were four to six lanes of traffic on just about all major highways. The only traffic jams I saw at Saturn were at the start or end of the shift. They may last twenty minutes at the most."

"However, in Atlanta, traffic was just something we had to adjust too. It was not a reason to be late for work. The first week, we spent a few hours a day in class where I met three other guys that I still keep in touch with. We had been talking about checking out Strokes, a strip club outside Atlanta. We met another guy that worked there when we went out for a break. He offered to show us the town that night. We all had cash. GM had just given us a big moving bonus. That night we all met up and hit about four strip clubs. It got to the point, if you have seen one, you have seen them all. Girls in one club were young enough to send you to jail. A few years later someone did go. You could tell the girls were not old enough by just looking at them.

We left and went to another club downtown and it was too loud after fifteen minutes I was ready to go. We stayed about an hour. When most men go to strip clubs they not looking for love. In my opinion, they're going to see what kinds of tricks a woman can do with her body. Just her being nude dancing and doing all kind of tricks for money, showing anything and everything is not love. I was not a night person and just wanted to go to bed so; I decided we should head home; it was 2:00 a.m.

I was in Atlanta living alone and going back and forth to Tennessee to visit my wife and kids who were coming at the end of the school year. On one visit, my two sons came back to Atlanta with me for the week that there were out of school.  On the trip back we stopped at a rest stop at the top of the mountain in Chattanooga Tennessee on interstate 24.  My oldest son and I went to rest area restroom while my youngest slept in the back seat.  It was close to midnight and we had about 5 hours to go before we made it home. We finished in the rest room, returned to the car, and got back on the road. After driving another 100 miles or so I needed to stop again, we were down the mountain and just about to the Georgia border.  I pulled up to the rest area and went to get out when my son said daddy, Drey not back there.  I looked and my youngest son was gone.  I asked my son but he had no idea where he was.  I told him to get in and we hopped back in the car and headed back up the mountain.  I call 911 on the way up and they were no help because I had no idea where I was.  I was going over 80mph most of the trip hoping I get stopped and get some help.  The trip back up was a lot shorter and I stopped on the side of the road and told my oldest son to go down to the next exit and come back to the rest area. I jumped the cement wall and ran to the building to find my son standing in front with a white woman eating a bag of chips.

He had gotten out of the car while we were in the bathroom to go to the snack machines and I never noticed.  I found out he had called his mom, and the police had been there and had also called her and said they had told him to stay there that I should be back when I notice him missing.  Then my cell phone rang, it was my wife; she wanted to know what was going on, and that the police in Tennessee had called her.  I tried to play it off like it was no big deal but when she found out I had left her baby alone on top of the mountain for almost 3 hours she went off making it sound a lot worse than it was. She stated what could have happened; told her what happen was me and Nat went to bathroom and he went for snack; he had been under a big blanket and we didn't notice he got out the back seat because it still look full to me.

When the line started, they expected you to be on your job. I was putting in the left axle.  It weighted about 20 pounds and I had to put a cater key in the ball joint then put the axel and nut in the side of the transmission.  I was doing about fifty-five an hour; add that up to 40 hours a week. I was in good shape but that would not last long. At that pace, the joints in my arms started to give out.

There were days when I had to switch from arm to arm. In addition, going to the doctor at work was just not helping. After about twenty-two visits about my arm in two years, I was sent for a MRI. It showed that a muscle was torn and I needed an operation to fix it.

The doctor that did the operation said I waited too long, and that the muscle was too far-gone. Now, I have a wire and a screw in my elbow that limits what I can do. The doctor at work had given me a band to wear and had always sent me back to work. Now that he saw that I did have a problem, he trying to blame me.

He was saying that I did not wear the band enough at work. The job would not cause that kind of injury. Another doctor told me that my arm needs rest and that I should have been taken off the job soon as pain started. That it may have saved the muscle. I checked with the person that did the job on the other shift and he was having elbow problems too. He had just started the job and said the other person was on sick leave.

I think the doctor knew he fuck up because I came back to work with no job to do. I was told to hang around and help if need. That lasted four months and I got bored fast. I ended up in the back of the plant doing almost nothing for about a year. My arm got better, but not 100%. I still did street work but nowhere near, what I did before I got hurt. I was just glad to be back at work; hoping my arm gets better soon.

My twin came to visit around 2003 in Atlanta. I had been telling him that it would be easy to do mechanic work here. I had to cut back because of my arm. We went to a Wal-Mart to get gas; as he filled the tank, I noticed a man with his hood up on a Range Rover. He reminded me of Braxton from The Jamie Fox show. Water seemed to be leaking from the front of the truck. I go over and introduce myself. I looked at the motor and tell him he needs to call a tow truck, or ruin the motor. I showed him the water pump. I tell him its shot and putting water in it will not do any good at that point. I tell him it must have been leaking for a while for it to tear up the bearings and throw the belt off. My twin finished the gas, came over to where we were, and looked at the truck.

I pointed out that the pump sits right in front of motor and easy to change. He asked if we could do it. I look at my brother and he nods. I said sure, he says how much and I tell him 100 dollars. He says I will give you two. We had him pull the truck out in the parking lot. My brother took the pump out while I took him to get the parts from the dealer. The whole job took about forty-five minutes and he gave us ten twenties. I gave him my number and his brother and some other friends called me for work a few weeks later.

I spent a lot of time with Kerry. He was my first real white friend. I am not going to say he is not prejudice. He is not against black and white but against stupidity. He treated everyone the same until you do something stupid and he will let you know, especially is he has been drinking.

I first started hanging out with Kerry when we were at Saturn. He invited me and another guy named Tim to a divorce party his friend Ron was giving after work one night. Ron has since passed from cancer a few years back. Tim and I were the only two black people there. Kerry and I, we are both from Flint Michigan and still had family there. He has gotten to know my family and I have got to know his. We made a few trips to Flint together. On one trip, that we made we stopped to eat somewhere on the highway about an hour south of Cincinnati. As we were eating, Kerry looked over and yelled, "What the fuck yall looking at!" I noticed that I am the only black person in there. Neither one of us had thought about it before or cared. He lost his appetite as he started to stare at the folks; who would quickly look away. I was ready to go and Kerry was not eating anymore. We were just about finished away. I think Kerry sat there chatting with me for another 30 minutes just to fuck with them and show the he can stare too. He took me to a Toby Keith concert on the Nashville riverfront with his daughter and her boyfriend. It was off the hook even though we had driven from Atlanta that evening, we were both tired. They have a mechanical bull that people would line up and pay to ride. Beer was everywhere. Kerry was feeling no pain. I did not drink so I just keep my eyes on him. Somehow, we managed to drop off kids and hit the road heading to Texas.

# "20. JAILHOUSE VISIT"

Around 2004, one of my younger relatives got in a lot of trouble and was in jail In Atlanta. I had told her I would visit before I went to work one day. I had to make a trip on that side of town anyway. I did my running around and by 1p.m., I still had time to go to the jail to visit her before I had to be at the plant at 4:00p.m. The jail is on I-285 and Memorial. When I got there I parked and went in after talking shit with her for about forty-five minutes, I told her to keep her head up. Then I said, "Goodbye."

As I went out of the front door and walked to my truck I looked up at the parking lot on hill where I had parked and froze. There were cops at my truck, at least three. I turned around and pulled out my phone and put it up to my ear. Boy, I was wet with sweat and shaking all over. I leaned against a tree like I am on the phone with my back to my truck. I look around and could see cops all around. I saw the helicopter blades are turning. The helicopter always sat there where you can see it from I-285. I didn't look at my truck. I had the phone up to ear. I don't want to look dumb standing there. I saw a city bus going by then I noticed a bench.

I don't see anyone looking at me. I have been waiting for cops to walk toward me; so far nothing has happen. I decided to go sit on the bench and wait for the next bus. Then I call Kerry to come get me.

I took one fast glance at the truck and noticed there were five cops now three in blues and two plain clothes. Something was strange. They were not at my truck but the one next to it. I stopped and turned so I could get a good look. It seemed that someone had locked his keys in the truck next to mine. The others were trying to help him. It was a late 90's GM ex cab pickup truck. I put my phone back on my belt and walked over. My shirt still wet, but I am calm now."

"Two of the cops were white and three in blues were black and were leaning on my truck. One cop was telling the others about the young pussy he had seen in the club where he was moonlighting at the night before. The two white cops were trying to get the keys out. I asked them to let me try and that I was on my way to work at

General Motors. I had worked at the truck plant in Flint too. I went to my toolbox and got a long rod and a screwdriver. It took me about three minutes to pop the window and get a rod in to push the lock button.

He was so happy! He offered to pay me but I told him I was fine. As soon as the door opened the three black cops walked away. The other white cop got in their car one space over and left. The one that owned the truck offered to buy my lunch. I told him I was fine. I had to get to work at the plant. He made a few more offers to give me something but I told him it was cool. I stood back so he could back out. Then I put my tools back and went to driver side and got in. I took a deep breath reached over and patted the ounce of weed I had on the seat. I open the ashtray relit my blunt and drove home.

On the way, I called Kerry and told him I had the mail. He knew what that meant and had already paid his postage. I asked if he wanted to meet me before work or after. He said before was good. I was still thinking about what just happened. When Kerry got there I told him about the police. We had a good laugh. Saying if only the cops knew what was on the seat I would be off work for a minute. We both knew with Atlanta drug laws that it would have been a hard hit. The cops there will get you for the scent of smoke in your ride.

We sat and smoked till it was time to go to work. At lunch, as we sat out back in our friend van, I told them the story again. They all said I should have taken the cash or lunch or a get out of jail free card.

The next week as I was coming to the plant Kerry met me in the parking lot and says cop and dogs at the door checking lunch boxes and stood in front to stop me. I am clean mailman. He did not run today. He turned and walked in with me. We got to the door I was like Damn! Cop and dogs are all in black. It looked like they were on a real raid at a real dope house. It was summer time in Atlanta. I know they were hot with all that shit on, even the poor little dog had on a vest. I always thought police dogs were big, but I guess they can be any size long as they can smell dope.

They came up and down the line going from locker to locker. If the dog got a hit, he would sit down by the locker. Well he sat down by our utility man desk and looks at his handler. We knew Johnny drank a little, but that's it. We could not wait to see what the dog had found.     The line was still running and a lot of folks were trying to see. When they opened the desk and starting sifting things out and looking through them, it took them about 15 minutes to focus on a job bottle with a little in the corner. They clowned Johnny for the rest of the week about the dog the cop and his job. This did put an end to bringing anything on to GM property. The cops may act like a joke sometime, but we know they have to be serious."

# "21. MOVING TO TEXAS"

The van plant announced that it was closing by 2009. Anyone that wanted to go to other plants can leave. They offered $67,000 over three years to move. I put in to go the Hummer plant in Shreveport, Louisiana. Just before I sign the final papers, I saw that Texas was on the list. I had kinfolk there so I switched.

I had been to Texas a few years before. All I knew it was hot and flat. I came to town about three weeks before I had to be there to look around and check out the town. My twin met me in Arlington. He had lived there years ago after getting out of Army. Now he was working at Union Pacific Railroad in Little Rock. He had been off due to an injury and, He did not know when he was going back to work. We looked around the town, after a few days I headed home, after I had found a place to live. And He went back to Arkansas.

I was just about home when he called, and said that his job had just called and offered him a job in Arlington; the same GM plant that I was going too. It was hard to believe. I started in October 2006 and he got there in February 2007. He works at the gate at the GM shipping yard for Union Pacific railroad. Shipping out the cars we build.

There was no way for us to plan it that way, but it could not have turned out better. We lived in the same apartment complex for a while. We also still did light jobs in the streets sometimes.

When I got to Texas the work at the truck plant was all work. The days of doubling up and sweeping were long gone. There were bells, lights, and buzzers on just about every job. You had to check and verify that your co–workers had done their job. If they missed, something and you were the one looking to see if they put the part or plug in. and if you missed it too. It may find you in the labor relation office.

The workers here worked in teams and had meetings every week on what's going on in and around the plant. The also voted that all employees not driving GM car or trucks must park out near the street or risk getting towed. In some plants, I worked at years ago you would only see GM rides, because no foreign cars were allowed to park in GM lot at all.

I decided to go check out the police auction in Dallas Texas. I was not looking for anything just wanted to see what they had. I always get a bid number just in case I see something. When I got there, the crowd was somewhat big. That is not a good sign to me. I was late and they were on the second row already. As I walked up they were selling a big motorcycle. The bid was at $600. I looked around not knowing much about motorcycles. However, I knew it was worth a lot more than that. The next thing I knew my hand was up and up again beating the next three bids. When the woman looks at me and says, "Sold for $900."

I took a good look at the bike. It was a 1989 Honda Gold Wing 1500 with the v 6 motor and reverse. It had been dropped on the left side, and the oil had come out though a large crack in the motor. I took it home and got online looking for parts.

After finding all I could about the bike, I figured I could get about three grand for it. I took a picture and took it to motorcycle shop in Richardson, Texas. I told him what I needed, and he said he could get it all for about $300. Before I left, I showed him the picture. I was going to fix it, and try to sell it for three grand. He looked at the picture and said you may want to double your price. Later I found out that it was kind of like the caddy of bikes. Next to Harley that is

I still planned to sell the bike. I spent weeks on eBay looking for parts and reading about the bike. On the day, I got it all done and took a ride around my building. It ran better than I thought it would. It was so easy to ride, and had music and a windshield.

I had owned bikes before but nothing like this. I decided to go around the block. Texas is a helmet if you want to state. I still had my black work rag tied around my head.

With the music blasting as I came around the corner on the Watson Road service drive. The bike seemed to lean toward the on ramp to highway 360. Next thing I knew, I was going 75mph. and I knew I was keeping it. There is nothing like being out in the open air on a bike. There is always the fear of going down. I guess you really don't think about it until you fall or crash.

I never knew what I was missing. It seem that the bike talked to me when we out on the road. One day I asked, my girl if she wanted a ride. She said just around the building. I said ok. She got on and we were off. As I went past the gate, it was open so I hit the gas and we shot out in the street. I heard her say something but I just kept going. She tapped me on the back. I turned the music up and just smiled. What could she do from back there? We made the light and were on the main road. I pulled into a gas station and stopped. I got off expecting her to be pissed she smiled. And said I could have let her know I was going on the streets. I said it was the bike pulling me out. It's ready for the open road.

I asked, "How she liked the ride?" "Ok," she asked, "do I get my own helmet? "We will see," I said. As we got on the bike to go home, she said, "that I need to slow down a little." "I could have sworn that I heard the bike say back that she needs to stop screaming like a bitch." Maybe it was just the music.

I go to lots of yard sales and auctions. You never know what you may find. At a rummage sale, I got a small drum. It turns out to be about four hundred years old. It is a Turkish Ottoman Kettle Drum. It is in good shape and I sent info about it to a museum. They wanted me to send the drum after seeing the pictures they asked for. I told them was not willing to mail it. I asked if there was anywhere in Dallas that can look at it. They sent me a list of places that they said would be able to tell me more about it. Looking over the list, all the places were out of state. I did not think about sending it anywhere but back in the bag my lady's coach purse came in. That is where it is today.

After being here a year, I am learning to love Texas. I get to where I need and want to go. At the plant, there have been rumors that GM and the Union talking are going bad and the plant may strike. I paid close attention this time. The news was on it. Not as bad as when I was back in Flint. Every day for about a week before we walked out there was something about GM and the Union on the news.

On the day, we walked there were news trucks parked across the street and a few choppers in the sky. The strike was short and settled soon. The deal was not what the Union wanted for the workers but one we could live with.

Over the years, the unions have given up all kinds of benefits just to keep plants open. I am sure they will go as close to selling their soul as they can to keep workers on the lines. I wish the union would help with my problems.

My arm is getting sore and I have to put the bike up for a while. Soon I am unable to work and find myself on workers compensation. I was unable to keep up with the line; with my hand, swelling up all the time. Riding the bike was getting so painful and I sold it for a good price. If I can't ride it I don't want to see it.

There is a deal on the table that will allow me to retire with thirty years, on June 1, 2009 and if god bless me to make it that far. That's what I will do. It seemed like the time I been working for is here, at forty-nine I have did thirty years. I have been looking at older men with lots of seniority sit around for years on gravy jobs. Before I knew it, my thirty years were up and no gravy job came my way. I was on the line down to my last day that I worked. I was unable to keep up with the line. It was suggested that I retire when the next deal was on the table.

I was in no shape to complain and after thirty years and two operations on my elbow. I just could not keep up with the line at about 550 jobs a day.

I spent my last two years on and off sick leave with arm problems. The doctors said my joints were worn out from thirty years of repetitive use. GM doctors say its old age.

I went back to work for three weeks in 2007. The first two I was on light duty and did have arm problems but kept it to myself. Then I was sent, to the line where I found I could no longer keep up with the line. My hand seems to stay swollen and had a numb feeling.

I had begged the doctor to let me go back to work to try and work my last year. He told me that he did not think it was a good idea and that the arm would not get better but he gave in and sent me back. Now, I see he was right, by Wednesday of the third week I could no longer pretend that I was not in pain. I could not hold the tools or the parts. I stayed in the hole. There were bells and lights going off every time I went too far down the line. It was just more than I could handle. The pain pills were not doing any good. I was not supposed to take them at work, but I had no choice. First aid had done all they could. Seeing how swollen my hands were, I was sent home. There was just so much that icy hot cream can do.

I took a much needed rest and used my hand as little as possible. The numb feelings had been in my fingers for months now, I guess I will just sit and Take care of my arm and wait for June 09 to get here.

# "22. MECHANIC PARTS AND LABOR"

Being a mechanic is a very dangerous job. I don't care how good you are. Safety should be the first thing on your mind before you touch or attempt to repair a vehicle. You need to know if it's in a safe place to be worked on. Is the engine hot? Do you have to jack it up? Do you have jack stands? Do you have gloves to protect your hands? Do you have the right tools? And do you know what you're doing?

There are many kinds of mechanics. Some are honest some not so honest. It's good to know as much as you can about your car and the problems you are having before you call a mechanic. It is easy to be cheated or overcharged if you have no idea what is being fixed. Some mechanics can pay for their vacation on one job, by telling you anything and selling you something you don't need. Most mechanics are honest but you still need to know your car.

There are hundreds of problems you can have with a car or any truck. You also have lemons and recalls. The difference in my opinion is one is caused by workers and the other is by the maker or designer. It's like this, 50,000 cars are built. If 5,000 keep going back to the dealer for repairs they are lemons. They may were built on a party day near weekend. If all 50,000 go back it's a recall. Now I don't really mean a party night, but a night that the plant will be out for a long weekend leading into a holiday or some time off.

There hundreds of departments on the line from start to finish of building a car. If on the last night to work all the department have dinners, and there will be some drinking. There will also be people that took that extra vacation day at that time or just didn't come in. Their job will have to be covered by someone not familiar with that job. That could be hundreds of people, and if just a few are not able to do their job on the same night and miss parts or miss the night, that may cause a group of lemons. Those cars may take trip after trip back to the dealer. Any time the regular job operator is not on the job or his in his right mind, there a better chance of missing a part and causing repairs or problems. Most workers have at least three or four things to do on all cars or trucks or whatever is coming down the line. And it's easy to miss something if you are not careful.

Most shops charge you by the hour. The price range varies depending on the type of car and work to be done. Mechanics at shops make good money, but mechanics can make better money doing side jobs. They can charge labor outside the shop on some jobs for less money.

The most important thing for a mechanic is to have good tools. Cheap tools can do a lot more harm than good. They can be very dangerous. Most of my tools are Sears Craftsman. They last forever, unless you lose them. Sears will replace any tool you may break or damage. A good place to get tools, are at yard sales on a Friday or Saturday morning. Most sellers don't even look at the brand they just sell it for a dollar or two unless they know tools. You can find just about anything you are looking for at yard sales in the summer time, from tools to baby clothes at pennies on the dollar.

There tools for everything on a car. There are also some special tools that are needed for some jobs. Having the right tool means getting the job done faster and safe. A mechanic must have tools for just about every job that they are called for. Tools for special jobs can also be rented at places like AutoZone and O'Reilly's.

It only takes one thing to stop a car or truck from running. There may be many things leading up to the failure until just one thing just gives out. Preventive care is the best way to avoid high repair bills. There are some things you just don't replace or think about until they break. Some states have emissions and inspections before they can be tagged. The years I lived in Flint, Michigan, there weren't any inspections or emissions. All you need was tags and insurance to drive. They didn't care what the car looked like or if it was safe to drive.

With the computer world as it is today, you can get online and do a lot of research on whatever you are working on. There are websites on all cars where people share information on car repair and parts. Websites on aftermarket parts can be found online, and parts can be shipped from anywhere to anywhere. One of the best sources of parts is the junk yard. Salvage yards or an auto recycling company are basically all the same thing.

Mechanics work on cars has changed a lot in my thirty plus years in this kind of work. The basic operation of vehicles is the same.

Now you almost need a computer to work on some cars. There are some onboard computers controls that are way over the head of some us street mechanics. If I had to go to school, again I am not sure I could pass all the tests of today's auto repairs. Some mechanics only deal with one kind of car or have a specialty like brakes or air condition charge.

Cars from thirty years ago were built a lot heavier and with bigger motors. Their bodies were steel and could be bumped and bonded back in shape if dented. They were easy to work on because there was less under the hood to work with. Back then, you only needed about three or four difference size wrenches to work on any car or trucks. Now you need special tools to do some jobs.

Most mechanics don't work on modified motors that are fixed for racing or anything other than normal driving. They also don't like working on cars where someone has jerry rigged shit under the hood or that have shit hotwired everywhere.

The first thing a mechanic should do on a car less than three years old is ask owner about the warranty. If there is one, it should go to the dealer or whoever is covering it first, so it won't be voided.

In Atlanta, you see mechanics outside some auto parts stores offering to help you for a few dollars. They only do simple jobs take minutes, like headlights or wipers if the stores don't offer to do it. I have seen some do tune-ups and brakes. The stores don't seem to mind and I have seen them send people out to see a mechanic in the lot.

In Michigan the biggest problem I saw was rust, even if a car has been rust proofed it was still hard for mechanic to work in some areas like the gas and brake lines because the rust can eat through anywhere. You may do more damage trying to fix a leak and end up replacing a lot more than you started doing. A car that is about 7 years or older is ready for nuts and bolts because it is rusty and frozen in the underbody, and anywhere else salty water and ice can sit and rust

Some street mechanics will do just about any small job for ten to forty dollars. Enough to get something to drink eat and smoke. Others take the job more serious. A good street mechanic can pretty much tell a problem by sound of car or the owner telling about problems they are having.

It's hard to find a street mechanic that will work on foreign cars like Jags, Benz's, and BMW's. Working on these cars cost more and some need special tools. You also have to know what you're doing. One wrong setting of something like a timing chain can destroy the motor. There are a lot of thing that a weekend mechanic should not do, and should be left to the pros. As street mechanics get older they learn what cars not to touch, because the money not worth the stress and strain the work may cause.

Most street mechanics cannot walk past someone with an open hood having problems. Something in them make them want to help, some see money. Some just wanna show how much they know, and some really wanna help.

Sometime, it is hard to explain to someone why it cost four hundred dollars to put on a twenty-dollar part. The motor may have to be lifted or taken apart. There also may be other parts that have to be replaced if removed. Cars are like a big puzzle and the key to repairing them is to know what the parts are and where all the pieces go.

There are a lot of places to get good used parts if you know what you are looking for. Some salvage yards have computerized systems to tell you if they have the parts you need. Some used parts are as good as new and you get a better price if you take them off yourself. You have to be sure that you are getting the right part because most places are no cash back, just exchange. Most places have a thirty day warranty on used parts. If it's bad you should know within thirty days. Some junkyards in Texas have meal wagons set up out front. Some have men selling tools and sometimes men set by the entrance offering to pull parts for you.

There are also a lot of websites where you can look for parts, or search car problems. It's also good to keep a good record of all that is done to your car while you own it. There are many things that an owner can do to repair their own car but there are some things that must go to a real mechanic.

I suggest you get to know your car or truck and to check the oil and water. Along with anything else that the car manuals suggest you do. If you treat it right, it will treat you right.

I remember my first day in mechanics school. The teacher said we would make most of our money from women. That was in 1988 and I found it to be true then and still today. He said that if you

show a woman ten things she needs to fix.  She will fix as much as
she can pay for.  Men will do just enough to keep it on the road

# "23. RETIRED, DIVORCED, AND DATING"

My clock at GERERAL MOTORS stopped at 12:01 am June 22 2009. I end my years at general motors the same way I started, single. I find being retired at 50 is very boring. I keep myself busy working on friends cars or on the road going somewhere. I thank god for the skills I learned over the 30 years that I was employed at GM, and for allowing me to walk away with my mind still in place.

I would be lying if I said all GM workers were happy and gave 100 percent. Like in any other job .There were some that just wanted the money and have nothing to do with the union or anything that don't have anything to do with the line. To them it was all about work. They just want to just do their time and go home.

They did not deal with the potluck dinners that some teams have or share their family stories. I have worked with people that if a shooting was to happen I would put them first on the list to do it.

30 years is a long time on one job and there are thousands of people all over the world that have done it. There are also thousands of people that have started on 30 years and for some reason did not make it. There are lots of reasons to leave GM like layoffs, buyouts early retirement, or just to find something else to do. I believe everyone that started out really thought they could do 30 years and out. But time and your body can change your mind and some people start to look for a way out and look at any offers GM have at the time.

Which there are few of at any time unless GM has a lot of people they need to get rid of? I had been working a long time before I got to GM and seems like I will be working long after. Sometime people just seen to turn into what they do for a living, and Being a mechanic seem to be the perfect job for me

There were many days that I wanted to quit and find something else to do, but with no college, it would be hard to find a job making GM kind of money. I have worked on the line with people that have college degrees and still make more money on the line. Now I thank God I stuck it out to see what the end of 30 years would bring.

If I had to do it all over again, I would, but knowing what I know now, I would change a lot. I would work harder on my marriage.

Then again maybe it was never meant to be. I do thank God for my 2 boys my daughter and my grandbaby

I miss getting up at 5am and often find myself up at that time anyway. I lose track of days and seem like I have nothing to look forward too. I know that I have to find something else to do just to keep from going crazy. I see many older men working in places like Kroger and greetings people at Wal-Mart. I wonder if they need the job or just getting out of the house. To keep from going crazy or driving someone else crazy, maybe both.

Being retired also let me go home to West Helena Ark more. I try to go during football season so I can see my nephew play for my old high school. We went to the state championship game a few years ago, and in spite losing it was good to see 100 % of the town's people support the team and about 30% of them followed the team to the big game in Little Rock.

I went back to FLINT MI lately and was surprised at the conditions of the city mainly the north side. It seem like on all the streets in every block there were empty houses. Some were in bad shape falling down some burned out and some just empty. A few were boarded up but just a few. Most streets had big pot holes and I feel sorry for the drivers that hit them all day long. Hitting potholed causes damaged to the chasses and the steering parts to cars. It will be hard to sue because the line will be very long with all the potholes there. Stores are closed all up and down Saginaw Street that used to be booming when Buick was up and running. I see people moving out of flint to the surrounding townships. Where new homes are being built all over the area

It's not all bad. I see Flintstones showing the rest of the country they can make it. I see some new stores and people working on some of the homes. If Flint can get a good leader I see them bouncing back .GM did hurt Flint, but it did not kill it. I also see some places that have been there for years and the ups and downs of Flint don't seem to affect them. Like beer wine and liquor stores. If they were there in the 80s most of them are still there. Also the churches seem to be getting bigger and the members younger. For every child you read about in the paper doing something wrong. There are thousands doing good that you hear very little about because that's not news, it's just life.

I have seen many fads come and go from high top fade to the micro weave, some good some bad. And in my opinion the worse fad to date is the young men with their pants below their ass. Like they in a contest to see who can get them the lowest. It's just something I will never understand, and neither would my mother.

I saw 30 years of change not only in the plants but in the world with the coming of computers and cell phones. That bring a whole new way of living that some people seem to can't live without. Gone are the days for paper maps now we got GPS that supposed to talk you though to your destination. With new laws that come along with them. Pictures can be sent anywhere in minutes and not have to be sent out by a store to be developed, unless you're old school. Lots of print shops have gone out of business because it's easy to do things a home on a computer.

I find myself going days sometimes weeks before I get a haircut of shave. With no lady at the time, I can just be me, long as I am clean. Having the crack head look does not bother me and I see no reason to get haircut and shave if nowhere to go.

I don't have much patience for women now, and spend lot of time alone or working. I was invited out to have a drink with a lady I met online. We had been talking on the phone and online for about a month. This was my first time getting to meet her face to face. I wanted to see what she looked like. We met at Applebee's for dinner. I got there first, and sit out front waiting. She was late, now I thinking that, I was stood up. After about 20 minutes, I saw a nice looking lady walking up to the door. She came in looked at me and called my name. I got up and gave her a hug. She was a lot better looking than I expected. I had already put my name on the list and we went right to our seats.

We did small chat as we waited to order. I got a good look at her, fake nails, fake hair, no bra, nipples about to pop out, and too much makeup for me, fake eye lashes. In addition, jean so tight I wonder if she having trouble breathing.

She was telling me about the kind of man she like, and what she wants him to do for her. I was just looking at her talking about having a real man with all that fake shit on. I was getting a little bored with her and was hoping dinner would hurry up and get there so we could just eat. She keep talking and talking. I look at her mouth and it's just moving. She is talking about everything that has to do with what she wants in life and in a man.

I say, look I not looking for a love connection, so whatever we going to do we can do tonight. In addition, I got a lady friend in north Dallas and I am keeping her. She looked at me as if I lost my mind and said you get right to the point don't you. I say, I don't want to waste my time or yours. And I am too old to be the kind of man you want. Our dinner came and as we ate, she did not talk much but she kept looking at me. Thinking the night was a wrap, all I had to do was finish the meal. Then I could get back to my home. She was not bad company at all and very sexy, she was just hooked on herself. Now there is nothing wrong with that, if you got the time, which I don't. After dinner, we just sat for a while and went to her car to talk some more while she smoked. She said, my lips looked soft and asked for a kiss. She asked me if anyone ever told me I look like Samuel Jackson. I told her that is all I hear, sometime it get on my nerves when people bring that up. I told her about a clown that hit me up in a store one night. A real clown, he said he was coming from doing a show in Dallas somewhere. He gave me his card, and said I was a dead ringer for Jackson and could make big money in look a-like shows. He said to think about it and give him a call. Well if he looks like me, he owes me big money I would think. She said, I should call and see what it leads too.

We decided to go for a ride and she showed me her house. We sat in her driveway for a few minutes talking, with her telling me about her kids and big blue pit-bull dog. I was not going in; I was not ready to meet kids or a blue dog. She asked for another kiss.

Next thing I know we checking in to a hotel. We stayed until checkout the next day. The next morning she talked about where this was going .I was at lost for words at first .She was cool but I was not looking for love connection  as I had told her at dinner or girlfriend at that time. I had only been divorced for a few months .I was up front about that and a good night in bed was not going to change my mind. And she blew anything long term and turned herself into a booty call by sleeping with me on our first meeting. No telling how many men she met before she met me and did all of them get lucky?

It seems that there are so many pretty women that are single, that there should be about seven to every man. I think that a man should marry as many women as he can take care of, long as everybody is happy.

It seems hard to find someone that I can trust and feel relaxed with, and at my age, I just say what is on my mind. That way if I say something to make a woman mad I know right then and hope I don't have to worry about cut tires or broken windows. I just don't do drama with anyone about anyone else I see. If I don't put a ring on anyone's finger then I am single and free.

I try to get an understanding with any women I meet that I am not the boyfriend type. I stay in the street too much and most of the people I meet or work for are women. Not that I am fucking any of them, I just don't want anyone just sitting around waiting on me to finish working somewhere. Or upset when I am going to work for another lady. And I get the 20 questions when I get in.

I still keep in touch a few friends that I have known for years at GM. I go visit somebody every time I go to Flint Michigan or Atlanta GA.  GMs Face book  help me keep in touch. I also spend a lot of time just looking on a website called; Crag list. I saw an ad selling a BMW convertible that had motor problems. I went for a look and the guy sold it to me for 1000 dollars. After taking it home and spending 2 days, putting the motor in. I took it on a road trip to Arkansas and Atlanta. I miss my motorcycle and riding with top down was close but not the same.

I do hope my arm gets well enough for me to take a ride across the country on another Gold wing motorcycle or maybe a Harley, nothing like being on the open road, with the wind in my face, but I have to have a windshield bugs can blind you.

I don't know what the next 30 years will bring for the UAW and GM. I hope they continue to fight their way back to number one.

I don't know what the next 30 years will bring for me. I may write another book because, I do have more to tell, or just keep doing small jobs. I do plan to keep busy and travel as much as I can. I find many new doors open to me now that I have time to set back, look at my life and see which way to go. I know my bucket list is not done because I am still dreaming.

I pray whatever inside me that pushed me to finish this book will still be there on my next Project whatever it may be.

# "24. BACK HOME IN WEST HELENA"

I go back to Arkansas every chance I got over the last 35 years , to visit my mom and other family I still had there .The city has really changed a lot of the big companies like the Faust saw mill where daddy worked has closed, and weeds have taken over the lot. The soybean plant had closed after a big scandal where they lost millions of dollars and a few people went to jail. The casinos moved across the bridge to tunica in the early 90s ,it was rumored that they brought up the good restaurants and hotels in Helena and west Helena, closed them so folks will have to cross the river for a nice dinner and room. There was a super Wal-Mart that some people called Wally mall, built next to the strip mall that seem so small now.

Whenever I go to casino seem to be a lot of older folks sitting around ready to go but the ride they came with still got money to spend, so they wait. The casino did provide lots of jobs that were needed because field work was being done more and more by machine.

They did build a new hospital and high school gym after the old one burn down in the 80s, the night the cougars lost the homecoming game.

The town had made national news a few times like around 1997 when the chemical plant caught fire killing 3 firefighters, injuring many more and blowing poison smoke across the town, My mom lived about 4 miles from the plant and I kelp checking on her by phone from Tenn., as I watched the fire on the news. My little brother told me they all were good and they had been told to stay inside and close all windows and doors, like that's going to help stop the smoke or the smell.

Bobby brooks or the Helena sportswear company, where my mom had worked as a seamstress for years had long ago closed and the long building was in very bad shape and had been gutted by fire and parts had fallen down.

The only thing that seem to be unchanged are the liquor stores they seem to be the same every time I come home ,even though I don't drink at all I can't help but notice . There are more churches, most of them small and seem to be just starting out but few have been there long as I can remember. The ABC café, and just about everything else on the line has been torn down. The Brick House lounge in southland was still standing last time I saw it, but I wouldn't go in for fear it may fall down.

The hut on Washington Street where my family had our 1st reunion in the 60s was still standing and not in too bad shape to be so old.

Lots of the stores in downtown Helena have moved on and now just a few antique stores and some longtime store owners that are in it for the long run.

The blues festival is one of the high times of the year when I always try to go home .it's the one time that you never know who you will run into.  All the stores there are open if only for that weekend .The city built a stage at the end of Cherry Street and uses the levy for seating which seems to be working out great for the 3 or 4 events the town have per year.

The town may seem like a sleepy little place but they have big city problems. The one that came as a very big surprise to the town in 2011 was "Operation delta blues". The Feds raided the whole town .Seems the town had been under a fed watch for 4 yrs with undercover officers and phone taps. About 5 police officers and close to 80 more people were rounded up. My little brother called me early that morning saying he had been stopped on the Mississippi Bridge on his way to work, so a large convoy of police cars and other law enforcement vehicles could pass on the way to Helena and west Helena, they went right to the police station and took over. The rest of the day played out on CNN news, as I watched helicopters fly over the city, as the police did their job .They also found over 400 hundred thousand dollars at one house in Marianna. They also got money and drugs from places in other surrounding towns. Three guys that I grew up with were picked up, one right down the street from my mother. It seems that a few of the police officers were working both sides of the law and thought no one would find out.

Five police officers were picked up for helping the drug dealers move the drugs throughout the towns. I never thought there was that much money or drugs moving though the city .that would explain the rise in crime since my high school days.

The big floods of 2011 hit the town hard and keep all eyes on the levy in Helena, fearing it may give away and flood downtown since it was only yards away from the river .The water had not been that high in years and farmers lost a lot of crops in the fields close to the river banks. The casinos parking lot was under water and some of their buildings closed.

It was always ease going home and the more of my sibling there at the same time always made my mama happy .she was always glad to show off any of her kids to anyone .My baby sister lost her husband in 2013 around Thanksgiving and at the funeral my mama let her kids know that she wanted them all home for Christmas, which is something she had never done before, my step dad had already told me about her wish, when I called to check on her the week before. whenever I called home, I talk to him for a few minutes and he tell me what's really going on with her about her health and anything else he think we should know, because if I asked her she will say she is fine and won't complain about anything. Then he will put her on the phone.

All ten of us made it home for2013 Christmas plus about a dozen plus grandkids and plenty of cousins and friends, the house was full. Mama was glad to see Otis and got on him for not stopping by more. I thought mama would want to go to church and show us off, but she had no plans to leave the house and just wanted to stay home with all her kids, she has one brother that also made it. Her baby brother, Uncle Jessie passed from a stroke in the early 90s and his twin sister passed about 3 yrs ago.""

"" I was on my way to work on Feb. 28 2014 when I got a phone call from my baby sister, asking if my other brother had called me yet. I told her no and she told me that mama had died a little while ago .I could not say much, I just said ok, and I would get with her later. It took a minute for it to sink in. I sat at a gas station for a little while thinking about her. For some reason I thought about my father and the day I told my little sister he had died. I still remember her crying filling the house, but she sounded so calm when she told me about mama. She called home the most and I knew she was trying to be strong like mama would want all of us to be.

I called my kids and my cousin in Michigan and my girlfriend. I still went to work to keep my mind clear and after the word started to spread I got more phones calls from family and friends. When I got home "Rev Polk" a minister friend and choir director had fallen asleep on my sofa waiting to pray with me when I got in. After a short prayer with me, he asked about the service, I told him it would be in West Helena Arkansas the next week; he said that he was going.

The next few days were hard and the planning of her service was in the hands of my older sister and brother that was still living in West Helena .I called my brother and asked about Rev Polk singing if they had room on the program, if he is able to make it. After telling me he will get back with me on it, we talked about the other plans and about what my older sister had asked us to wear.

After getting to mama house I found it full of kin folks, and after making my way in halfway through the house my cousin, from Michigan comes up and gives me a hug, holding what I thought was a little girl until she asked him who I was and he said that's my papa, and then jumped into my arms and gave me a hug .He had just turned 3 and had about a foot of hair all over his head .I didn't remember him being so loud. After my twin came in he couldn't tell us apart so he just said he had 2 papas.

I had been taking with Larry Brown, the undertaker for our family in West Helena on Facebook before I left Texas heading for home. I have known Larry all my life. His parents lived next to my grandfather in Lexa, who had passed in 2002 after a stroke at 98. He lives right down the street from my mother and I knew he would take good care of her.

I never thought about my mother's funeral and was not sure how I or my other sibling would handle it. There were so many friends that I had not seen in years at her wake and after I saw her laying there I was at peace. She looked so peaceful and at rest that I could not be sad. The day had come that she had been living for. My mother did not just believe God is real, she knew he was, and had taught us to believe in him too. She had been at the same church over 40 years and was the longest serving member there. Her funeral was like a church reunion with so many people there from the past. Members of the class of 1978 were there to represent the class as were other classes that my other sibling were in ,all 10 of us  were central cougars

We kept a close eye on my step dad , we were glad that he had been there for almost 20 yrs with her after her 2nd husband died in

1988.We could tell he was taking it hard but he was more concerned for us. My brother had put Rev Polk on program to sing and he made it to town just before the service started. He sang "my soul is anchored in the lord "and did a great job that everyone enjoyed. He had to get right back on the road and go back to Texas for a prior engagement and left soon as the service was over before eating. My family could not thank him enough and 2 weeks later we gave him a dinner at my home to thank him.

We buried mama on highway 49 on a hill where the grass is kept cut and clean, unlike the old cemetery where my father and grandparents are buried, where it has gone unkempt for years. At the cemetery my brother joked with my step dad about the lot next to my mom being vacant. He laughed, and said he didn't need any land right now. Later that night we all sat around talking and looking though some of mama things , I never knew she had so many hats, all I wanted was one of her homemade quits, that we used to have to help with.

After getting back to Texas still thinking about mama, I talked to my step dad and he told me about finding mama on the floor in her room and after she whispered a few words to him then she had kind of waved and smiled then she was gone. I already knew most of it but it seems to help him to talk about her.  He told me that my other brothers and sisters had been calling to check on him.

The next week I got a call that he was on way to hospital ,and it may be a stroke .He managed to live a few days and then he was gone .It was then I found out how little I knew about him . He had one daughter that we never knew or saw before now and had lost son yrs ago and as far as I knew that was it .We were his family now that mama was gone, and I know she would want us to care for him as we did for her, which we had already planned to do.

We put him right next to my mother, which is the spot my brother had showed him at my mom's burial .I think when she waved to him she knew she would see him soon.

We all went back to the house after dinner to just hang out. we knew we had to do something with the house and content so we decided for the 10 of use to get whatever we wanted .all I really wanted was a quilt and after we got what we wanted the house was still full .so we opened up to grandkids and close friends selling the bigger things with no arguments at all, we just work and laugh as we went through the house, trying not to be sad.

The next few weeks were filled with heart pains, I had been taking BC headache power dally for months and was not getting better .I finally went to doctor and got a call when the test came back that they wanted to see me ASAP, and had already made an appointment for the next day .the doctor told me they had found serious heart problems and I needed to be treated right away. It seems that my heart was only working at about 40 % of what it should be and I was a walking heart attack.

I was put on 4 kinds of blood presser medicines and told to take it easy for a while .I knew I had to tell my sibling, the last thing we needed was another surprise. I sent them a mass text message telling them about my problem, some called and some texted me back, but I had their prayers and support.

I also texted my cousin in Michigan and a few minutes later my phone rang ,it was my cousin Shelia ,she was my age and after talking to her for a minute she said ,mama want to talk to you. Aunt Willie got on the phone, for someone over 80 years old she can still fuss and yell, not at all what I expected. she  started, with it time for me to sit my but down , that I work too much, I did my time with general motors and it time for me to sit down somewhere, that if I die tomorrow folks will find someone else to fix they cars  . All I could do was hold the phone and listen to her fuss at me for not taking care of myself; I knew she was right, I should have gone to the doctor months ago. After she was finished fussing which was longer than I expected, I got the message

With the next few months of rest and little work it didn't take long for my heart  to get back to almost 100% ,I still need to gain my weight back but for now I will watch my heart. I do small jobs for friends and family, and I am doing fine in South Dallas.

The city of west Helena has elected a new mayor I hope and pray he does what he said; he would do when he ran for office to help get the city back on track

I end with words from the preacher that taught my parents. That I still live by today

"LEARN SOMETHING EVERYWHERE YOU GO, IF IT AINT NOTHING BUT DON'T GO BACK THERE ANY

MORE"… ELDER JAMES WATSON… 1925…    2009   LATE
PASTOR OF   WATSON TEMPLE; COGIC LEXA, ARKANSAS

.

# EPILOGUE

I now live in Texas retired; out of the 10 of us 5 now live here with 3 brothers staying in Arkansas, one in VA and another sister, in Atlanta, we get together every chance we get; our main focus was our mom.  Who had passed suddenly in February 2014, and my step dad passing away weeks later.

We know she would not want us worrying about her, she had lived for the day she died and everyone that really knew her knew it.

Not sure what the future holds for me but whatever it is I will stay close to my brothers and sisters, And the rest of my large family and friends.

It took me a total of 5 years to finish this book, but something inside would not let me stop until finished and published. This book is a close copy of parts of my life that I wish to share with you, it could be 100% true or all false or mixed with lies, I will never tell.

I just thank God for allowing me to finish and hope you enjoyed reading, and for making GM part of my life.

I have to just take one day at a time. And get ready for my next 50 years

PREACHERS SON

www.ingramcontent.com/pod-product-compliance
Lightning Source LLC
Chambersburg PA
CBHW061753020426
42331CB00006B/1465